The Best of
Iqbal

The Best of Iqbal

Selected Ghazals and Nazms with their English Translation and in Roman Script also

Kuldip Salil

rajpal

Established 1912
100 Years of Excellence in Publishing
rajpal

₹ 475
ISBN : 9788170289227
Ist Edition : 2011, 8th Reprint : 2026

BEST OF IQBAL (Poetry) by Mohammad Iqbal
Selected and translated by Kuldip Salil
Printed at G.S. Offset, Delhi

RAJPAL & SONS
1590, Madarsa Road, Kashmere Gate, Delhi-110006
Phone : 011-23869812, 23865483, 23867791
website : www.rajpalpublishing.com
e-mail : sales@rajpalpublishing.com
www.facebook.com/rajpalandsons

Preface

Translating poetry from one language into another is a difficult, some would say, an impossible task. The challenge here is the challenge of being faithful to the original, and at the same time retaining at least some of its charm and beauty. It is not only the idea of original that is to be conveyed, but its soul, its strength, its poignancy and sweetness and, if possible, its rhythm and resonance should also reach the reader. The goal should be that in translation also it should read like poetry. And the challenge is particularly tough in the case of the ghazal. One of the ways I could think of meeting this challenge was to translate the verse in rhymed couplets, ensuring that the rhymes are not laboured. And wherever rhyming was not possible, it has been dispensed with.

After I translated Ghalib, and because the book was well received, I felt encouraged to undertake a translation of Iqbal's Urdu poetry. Although I had translated a few of his nazms and ghazals for an earlier anthology, an independent volume of Iqbal's poetry in English was, after my *Diwan-e-Ghalib: A Selection,* the next logical step in view of my great love and admiration for his poetry.

For the present volume, I have selected nazms and ghazals from all the four collections of Iqbal's poetry. The share of *Bang-e-Dara* is larger than that of the other three because I admire *Bang-e-Dara* the most. It is only a selection of Iqbal's Urdu poetry, and so, many important ones from his *Kuliyat* (Complete Works) have regrettably been left out and from some of the longer poems only excerpts have been taken.

A number of poems included in this volume have been, as far as I know, translated for the first time. Otherwise also, I have consulted very few translations. However, in my assessment of Iqbal's poetry and for writing about his life and times, I have consulted a large number of scholars. These include Maulvi Abdul Haq, Rafiq Zakaria, Mian Bashir Ahmed, Prof. Arberry, Mian Abdul Aziz, Prof. Sunder Das, Dr. Hira Lal Chopra, Dr. William Jordan, Iqbal Singh and M. A. Latif. I acknowledge my debt of gratitude to all of them.

I thank Prof. Khalid Ashraf, Prof. S.N. Sharma and Prof. Sadiq for reading through the manuscript and making valuable suggestions. Thanks are also due to Shri O.P. Sapra, Shri Rahul Gupta and Shri Mithuraj Dhusiya for helping me prepare the manuscript. Last but not the least, I thank my daughters Ritu and Sarika and my wife, the last especially, for giving me freedom to work on this book.

Kuldip Salil

Introduction

Mirza Ghalib (1797-1869) is generally considered to be the greatest Urdu poet, but while reading Iqbal, one sometimes wonders if this pride of place should not go to Iqbal. He is a truly great poet. It can be argued that if Nobel Prize had been awarded fairly, if it was free from linguistic, regional, political and ideological prejudices, Iqbal would have been an obvious choice. I strongly believe that a nation which has not produced a poet like Iqbal is singularly unlucky. For, few other poets have written poetry which can help man realize his hidden potential the way Iqbal's poetry does, and thus builds a nation on the shoulders of men of substance and strength that should be the envy of the world.

Mohammed Iqbal was born in Sialkot on 9th November in 1877. He came of a Kashmiri Sapru Brahmin family which had converted to Islam two generations earlier. It was his grandfather Mohammed Rafiq who had left his ancestral home in Kashmir for Sialkot. His father Nur Mohammed was a deeply religious man who earned his living by selling caps, which he stitched with his own hand. Nur Mohammed was God-fearing, led a pious life and prayed regularly five times a day. He had great love of learning and many scholarly friends gathered for discussion at his business premises. Iqbal took keen interest in these discussions. Nur Mohammed's advice to his son was never to forsake the path of the Prophet, and Iqbal adhered to this advice all his life.

Iqbal was put under the charge of an ascetic scholar Maulvi Mir Hasan, under whom he studied the basics of Islam. Apart from his education in a regular school, it was the Maulvi who gave Iqbal a firm grounding in Urdu, Persian and Arabic. A man of mystic bent of mind, he ingrained in Iqbal a humanistic vision which inspired the poet to take up the cause not only of the depressed and demoralized Muslims, but also to speak out for the oppressed and exploited everywhere. Iqbal was sent to the Scottish Mission School in Sialkot, and then to the Junior College of the same mission. He was married against his wishes to Karim Bibi, daughter of a rich man and three years older than him. He was then twenty years old. From this marriage he had a son and a daughter. The daughter died young.

Iqbal is said to have fallen deeply in love with a dancing girl, Amir, in Lahore. As against Karim Bibi, with whom his relations were never good, Iqbal found in Amir an intellectual companion, beautiful and well versed in Urdu. This infatuation with Amir, though short lived, had left him distraught for a while, because her mother would not allow Amir to meet Iqbal.

Though his relations with Karim Bibi were estranged, she continued to live with him even after he shifted to Lahore and took other wives. It was only later in life that she left him for her parental home. Her son Aftab, however, never forgave his father for his treatment of his mother. The relation between the father and son became so bad and Iqbal was so much upset, that he ultimately disinherited Aftab.

Iqbal took a Post-Graduate degree in Philosophy from Punjab University, Lahore in 1899. For some time, he taught at Oriental College and later worked in Government College, Lahore. As a student, Iqbal had the good fortune of meeting Sir Thomas Arnold, who taught him Philosophy. Arnold recognised Iqbal's exceptional talent and greatly encouraged him. He introduced Iqbal to all that is best and robust in western thought and initiated him into the modern method of critical studies. With the passage of time, the relationship between the teacher and taught grew very close and on retirement Arnold recommended that Iqbal take his place. And it was on Arnold's suggestion that Iqbal went to Europe for higher studies in 1905.

At this time, Iqbal's reputation as a poet was soaring high. There was a great national upsurge in the country and Lahore was its epicentre. Meetings and gatherings were held where people, young and old, discussed issues and debated ideas. One such occasion was the annual meeting of the Anjuman-e-Himayat-e-Islam in which Iqbal had started participating from 1899 when he was a student. He recited a new poem every year and soon became a rage with the Urdu loving audience, both Hindus and Muslims. And some of his couplets like :

ज़ाहिदे तंग-नज़र ने मुझे काफ़िर जाना
और काफ़िर ये समझता है मुसलमान हूँ मैं

For the narrow minded Muslims I am a Kafir
And the Kafirs think I am a Muslim

or

मज़हब नहीं सिखाता आपस में बैर रखना
हिंदी हैं हम, वतन है हिंदोस्ताँ हमारा

Religion can never teach hatred, it must be understood.
We belong to India, and are bound by a common motherhood

became a part of the common parlance. So powerful was his poetry that the audience would be moved to tears. *Makhzan,* the best known Urdu journal of the day, started giving him a place of prominence. 'Himalaya', his very first poem in *Makhzan*, created quite a stir and very soon he became famous all over the country.

Iqbal's sudden rise to fame created much heartburn among fellow poets especially in Lucknow and Delhi. They dubbed him as a rustic Punjabi and found fault with his language and imagery. They ridiculed, for instance, the opening line of his poem, 'Saqi'—"नशा पिलाकर गिराना तो सब को आता है" *(To intoxicate somebody and to see him fall is quite easy)*. What language is it, 'Nasha Pilakar?' his critics would chuckle. They even asked him to stop writing in Urdu. Iqbal responded to these critics in a long essay in *Makhzan*. He told them that as time passed, a language grew in range and usages, absorbing the expressions and nuances of various groups of readers. English is an obvious example of this widening range. Urdu, he said, could no longer be confined to the staircase of Jama Masjid of Delhi and Imam Bara of Lucknow. It is only by wider participation that languages have developed and grown. All this, however, had no effect on his critics who continued to criticize, even lampoon him. This led Iqbal to chide them by saying that when God wants to destroy a language, He produces unimaginative critics.

Perhaps the most celebrated feature of Iqbal's poetry, which has a very powerful and universal appeal, is that it seeks to rouse and raise man to his full potential. His poetrv is inspiring, invigorating, ennobling, uplifting, at times cajoling, even shaming, but always showing us what we are, what we ought to be and can be :

बेखबर, तू जौहरे-आईना-ए-अय्याम है
तू ज़माने में खुदा का आखरी पैग़ाम है

The final message of God on earth/you are the very essence of the age, O ignorant one, know your worth.

or

तू शाहीं है, परवाज़ है काम तेरा

You are the eagle created to scale the greatest height.

Iqbal is famous for his doctrine of *Khudi* (Selfhood). His poetry urges man to uplift his *Khudi* to such a level that God himself should come forward to fulfil his wish. It is a clarion call to arise, awake or be forever fallen, to quote Milton. In this, Iqbal reminds us of contemporaries like Vivekanand, whom he might or might not have met or read, and Nietzsche whom he had certainly read. Like all great men, Vivekanand is a complex figure, but the most practical and visible mantra that he preached was strength. For him, weakness is a sin, and playing football comes before praying to God.

For Iqbal, man is not a handful of dust, but divine. He is the architect of his own destiny. This doctrine of *Khudi* was new to the Muslim theologians. It jolted their straightjacketed thinking. *Khudi* implies self-assertion, self-realization, self-discipline, self-reliance and self-fulfilment. Human beings must keep evolving and approach godhood. The aim of human beings should be recognition, discovery, cultivation and assertion of their *Khudi*. Iqbal held that a tyrant's power could be countered only by power, and appeal to his good sense and morality is a sign of weakness—a weakness, the wages of which are death. He wanted us to *Live in the world like an eagle and die like an eagle*. He commended fortification of ego, which could be achieved through courage and strength and by perseverance against all odds. One should be supremely indifferent to all worldly reward in the pursuit of one's goal, and thus cultivate the ego.

The image of the eagle or the hawk appears repeatedly in Iqbal's poetry. They are ruthless birds, but in Iqbal, they become symbols of power and strength, symbol of lofty flight, symbols even of the contempt for the lowly earth.

In Iqbal's times most of the poetry was shallow in thought, had contrived elegance and tilted towards the sentimental. He had no sympathy at all for the art-for-art-sake school. The poet, he held, had a mission to perform and he wanted to use poetry to convey a coherent set of ideas. He was against poetry written for mere entertainment and superficial beauty. The goal of poetry for him was to make men of mettle and transform the nation. For him the responsibility for the decline of a nation lay with the nation itself. It followed that Muslims were themselves responsible for their sorry state. As he says, in *'Jawab-e-Shikva'*:

जिनको आता नहीं दुनियाँ में कोई फ़न, तुम हो
नहीं जिनको कोई परवा-ए-नशेमन, तुम हो

You are the ones who lack all skill.
You are the ones who for their abode care not.
and

फिरक़ाबंदी है कहीं और कहीं ज़ातें हैं
क्या ज़माने में पनपने की यही बातें हैं

You are divided among castes in various sects
Is this the way to flourish in the world?

Aware of the painful aspect of human condition in general, and the condition of Muslims, in particular, he analyses it and gives his own diagnosis for its amelioration. And this diagnosis is strength, fortitude, courage and self-belief.

He who does not believe in God is to the mullah a Kafir
He, who does not believe in himself, is worse than a Kafir

Life, he said, is an endeavour for freedom; the process of creation is still going on and man has to take his share in it. For Iqbal, thought without action is a disease; a book of philosophy not written with the blood of the human heart is a worthless heap of papers.

Iqbal and His Contemporaries

In the first half of the twentieth century, two Indians dominated the literary scene, Tagore and Iqbal. Interestingly, they present more a study in contrast than similarity. Tagore was a conformist, he looked for harmony; Iqbal was a rebel and wanted to create turbulence so that one could build anew. Tagore brought out the romantic in man, Iqbal looked for and brought out the heroic. If Tagore is a poet of feminine beauty and a lover of music, Iqbal is a poet of strength and his poetry has fire. Tagore was a great organizer and founded institutions like Shantiniketan, whereas paradoxically, Iqbal was easy-going, his interests were abstract and he did not relish practical work. Iqbal once wittily said, "Tagore preaches rest and practices action, I preach action and practice rest".

It is contended that Iqbal's philosophy of the self is borrowed from the Nietzsche's idea of the Superman. There is indeed some resemblance between the two. Both Iqbal and Nietzshe were against the thinking that negates life; both affirmed the importance of existence and action. Iqbal waged a philosophical warfare against the Iranian spirit of cold-bloodedness that cheats us of our Life. Nietzsche also accomplished something similar through his philosophy of Dionysus. Dionysus, said Nietzsche, is a symbol of life; even when it is cut to pieces it is born again and always returns from destruction. In spite of this similarity, however, there is a fundamental difference between Nietzsche and Iqbal. Religious Iqbal and anti-religious Nietzsche exclude each other as thinkers. Nietzsche, says Iqbal, had a glimpse of the ideal but his origin and aristocratic prejudice marred his whole vision. Nietzsche's Superman is an embodiment of will to power, he is creative. And religion, according to Nietzsche, is the worst enemy of the creative force; strength and toughness, Humanity and justice are decadent. For Iqbal, on the other hand, religion is a great force in the universe, and pity, justice and goodness are essential accompaniments to physical strength.

Themes in Iqbal

Love and beauty are dominant themes in Iqbal's poetry, as indeed they are in all Urdu poetry. There is a difference, however, between Iqbal and others. While Iqbal saw beauty in everything except the really ignoble, the beauty that moved him most was the beauty of power and perfection. Beauty is a mental experience and not a quality of things. This concept of beauty has given his poetry a robust manliness and vitality, which is singularly lacking in Oriental lyrical poetry. His poetic genius is such that he can write poetry which has great for its spontaneity, as well as, poetry, which has matchless artistry. And he can write poetry which has a blend of the both.

Having spent his early years in Sialkot, which is situated along the foothills of outer Himalayas, Iqbal showed early love for nature, which inspired a number of wonderful poems, 'Himalaya' being the first among them. In *'Ek Aarzoo'* (A Longing), he writes:

पानी को छू रही हो झुक-झुक के गुल की टहनी
जैसे हसीन कोई आईना देखता हो

The rose-bough bends and touches the water
Like a beautiful woman enamoured of her own face
in the mirror.

or

in the same poem, earlier :

लज़्ज़त सरोद की हो चिड़ियों के चहचहों में
चश्मों की शोरिशों में बाजा-सा बज रहा हो

The birds should sweetly sing, the cataracts fall
And fill the atmosphere with rapturous melody

Iqbal had a fine sense of the dramatic. In a number of poems, he builds tension or conflict in the first part of the poem to be resolved in the second. As Mustamsir Mir says, he weaves the plot of the poem arousing curiosity, dropping seemingly casual hints which prove prophetic, and strikes the master stroke at the end. A device that Iqbal employs to convey his meaning is dialogue among animals. Another feature of his poetry is ambiguity, a quality much valued in modern poetry. Iqbal's ambiguity lies in raising questions without providing final answers. He is one of the most serious thinkers of the modern times. Poetry and philosophy co-exist in Iqbal, and no philosophy has been able to provide final answer to the eternal problems of life and universe.

Iqbal's poetry is not only profound, it is also moving:

आखिर-ए-शब दीद के काबिल थी बिस्मिल की तड़प
सुबह-दम कोई अगर बाला ए-बाम आया तो क्या

As the night was ending, the condition of the wounded one
was indeed a sight to see
What if somebody comes now after the dawn has descended

And then where else one would find such disarming, straightforward poetry :

माना कि तेरे दीद के काबिल नहीं हूँ मैं
तू मेरा शौक़ देख, मेरा इंतज़ार देख

I am not worthy of your sight, I concede
But, pray, do appreciate my love, my wait

or

भरी बज़्म में राज़ की बात कह दी
बड़ा बेअदब हूँ सज़ा चाहता हूँ

In full assembly, I have revealed the secret
I lack all manners and must be punished for it

One of the qualities of a good couplet is that it becomes memorable and becomes a part of our daily discourse. Iqbal is perhaps the most quotable poet after Ghalib :

लाज़िम है दिल के पास रहे पासबान-अक़्ल
लेकिन कभी-कभी इसे तन्हा भी छोड़ दे

Good if the heart is accompanied by the mind
But let it sometime its own way find

or

नहीं बेगानगी अच्छी रफीक़े-राहे मंज़िल से
ठहर जा ऐ शरर हम भी तो आखिर मिटने वाले हैं

It is not proper to behave like a stranger to a fellow traveller, O friend
Wait a little, O spark, for I too am hastening towards my end

And although Iqbal is an intense poet of the soul, his poetry is not lacking in satire, even laughing satire :

उमीदे-ए-हूर ने सब कुछ सिखा रक्खा है वाइज़ को
ये हज़रत देखने में सीधे-सादे भोले-भाले हैं

The hope of getting the hours in heaven has taught the preacher everything
Apparently though, he is simple and innocent looking

Iqbal's poetry possesses a bewitching and incendiary lyricism, which gives winged beauty to his verses. For instance,

हुवेदा आज अपने ज़ख़्मे-पिन्हां करके छोड़ूंगा
लहू रो-रो के महफ़िल को गुलिस्ता करके छोड़ूंगा

I will not stop till I make my wounds bare
I will shed tears of blood and colour the mehfil red.

or

तू बचा-बचा के न रख इसे, तेरा आईना है वो आईना
कि शिकस्ता हो तो अज़ीज़तर है, निगाह-ए-आईनासाज़ में

Don't be too protective towards it, for such is your mirror
That if it's broken, it will be dearer to its maker

It is a lyricism at once captivating and a lyricism that lifts us to a plane higher than where we are used to living. However, lyricism in Iqbal, unlike the lyricism of some of the romantic poets, is closely aligned with and actually comes across as a criticism of life, that is, the real problems of existence. Lyricism lends longevity to poetry, but poetry cannot live on lyricism alone. It has to have imaginative awareness and must address the real problems of life. And if it can speak of creating a destiny out of dust, as Iqbal's poetry does, it acquires lasting significance. And as Iqbal Singh, quoting Iqbal's adaptation of Bhartihari, says his poetry has the softness of a petal and yet it can cut the heart of a diamond.

In Iqbal's hand, the familiar images and symbols of Persian and Urdu poetry have become charged with new meaning relevant to contemporary situation. The mirror of his sensibility could at once reflect the excitement of all our yesterdays and the intellectual and emotional tension of the world of today. He may take us on a tour of planetary heavens or hell, but his primary concern is always with the living reality.

Although ghazal has been the most popular and dominant form of Urdu poetry, in Iqbal's time, nazm was also coming into its own. It had, however, not yet attained a blend of artistic excellence and depth of thought, which it did in the hands of Iqbal. Iqbal is at once a poet both of the ghazal and the nazm, but his contribution to the latter is unique. Not only did he make the nazm a vehicle for his powerful thought, his nazm, too has the lilt and beauty of the ghazal. If the nazm has the intensity and force to jolt us into awareness, it has a tragic tinge too.

चमन से रोता हुआ मौसमे-बहार गया
शबाब सैर को आया था सोगवार गया

The spring-time departed from the garden, weeping
And the youth that for a stroll came, went into mourning

तमन्ना आबरू की हो अगर गुलज़ार-ए हस्ती में
तो कांटों से उलझकर ज़िदंगी करने की ख़ू कर ले

If you indeed wish to live with honour in life's garden
Side by side with the thorns let you learn to live

In fact, Iqbal very often obliterates the barriers between the nazm and the ghazal. In this context, one is apt to recall Ghalib's regret that ghazal was not an adequate medium for conveying his thought. Thus, when the noted critic, Abdul Qadir, compliments Iqbal's poetic genius by saying that Ghalib is reincarnated in Iqbal, it may have something to do with Iqbal finding and perfecting a form which Ghalib wanted to find.

Can Iqbal be called a people's poet like Pablo Neruda, Mayorvosky or Faiz Ahmed Faiz? He was not an advocate of the class war, but his sympathies definitely lay with the poor and the oppressed. Not even the greatest revolutionary poet has written a more strident couplet than:

जिस खेत से दहकान को मयस्सर न हो रोटी
उस खेत के हर खोशा-ए-गंदुम को जला दो

Burn every corn of wheat growing in the field
That provides not for the tiller's need

or

उठ्ठो मेरी दुनिया के ग़रीबों को जगा दो
काख़-ए-उमरा के दर-उ-दीवार हिला दो

Rise thou now and wake up the poor of the world
Shake from their foundations, the palaces of the rich

or

सुलतानी-ए-जम्हूर का आता है ज़माना
जो नकशे-कुहन तुमको नज़र आये मिटा दो

The age of the common man is approaching fast
Blot out all the emblems of the past that you sight

He was against both capitalism and communism, because he thought they clog the sources of spiritual energy and so, impoverish the soul, still he could write :

गया दौर-ए सरमायादारी गया
तमाशा दिखाकर मदारी गया

Out of steam has capitalism run
Out goes, the juggler, his tricks all gone

In this and in a number of other poems, the impact of the Bolshevik Revolution is easily discernable.

In 1905, Iqbal travelled to England for higher studies. He studied philosophy and passed out with distinction. From there he went to Germany and received a doctorate for his work *The Development of Metaphysics in Persia* from Munich University. In Europe, Iqbal met Atiya Faizi, who belonged to the famous Badrudin Tayyabji family. He admired Atiya and fell deeply in love with her, which she abundantly reciprocated. "I don't keep any thing from you; in fact I consider it a sin to do so," he wrote to her. Iqbal was a full-blooded man who enjoyed the company of women. His friend Abdul Majeed Salik tells us that Iqbal, sometimes visited the notorious Hira Mandi too in Lahore. Khalifa Abdul Hakeem, who is an authority on Iqbal, says that

Iqbal believed in taking a plunge in love. Even more than to Atiya, Iqbal lost his heart to twenty five year old German beauty Emma Wegenast, from whom he took lessons in German.

Iqbal qualified as a Barrister from Lincoln's Inn, London and was called to the Bar in 1908. While in Europe, Iqbal was so occupied with his studies that he got little time to write poetry. In fact, at one stage, he thought of giving up poetry altogether, calling it a "useless pastime." Instead, he wanted to be active in the overall upliftment of the Muslims. Two of his well-wishers, Sir Abdul Qadir and Sir Thomas Arnold happened to be in London at that time. They impressed upon Iqbal that the kind of poetry he was writing was not at all useless. In fact, they told him that it would contribute greatly to the well being of his country and community. Both of them recognized his genius, which they said must be used for the good of humanity. These two gentlemen ultimately persuaded him to change his mind.

So far, Iqbal had been writing poetry only in Urdu. While in England, once he was invited to dinner by a friend. The latter asked him to recite one of his compositions in Persian. Iqbal said that he had hardly written any poetry in Persian. Back from dinner, however, the request gave rise to a chain of thoughts in his mind and he lay in bed musing over the idea till early hours of the morning. In that state, he composed two ghazals in Persian, which he showed to Abdul Qadir, who greatly appreciated their beauty and excellence of diction. Iqbal for the first time realized that Persian opened up a new and better medium for communicating his ideas. After that he wrote mostly in Persian.

The three years in Europe opened up new horizons to Iqbal. He saw for himself the great material and scientific progress that Europe had made and understood why they have been able to rule such large parts of the world. At the same time, however, he saw the danger that Europe posed to the Eastern and Islamic culture. He saw also the superficial hedonism of leading circles in Europe and the growing gap between the ideals of Christianity—of charity and love—and the daily life of the individuals and communities. Capitalism had lost its progressive character and had become blatantly imperialistic. The nations of Europe were engaged in a fierce struggle against one another in their efforts to subjugate new territories. In this race, new alignments were being forged in which ethics and morality were the worst causality. Hypocrisy ruled the roost. Nationalism and patriotism were being used to occupy and exploit the backward nations of the world. This made Iqbal an opponent of the western idea of nationalism and democracy because of the hiatus between these concepts and their application by their practitioners. He was opposed to these ideas also, because he had a vision of Islam that should transcend national barriers. One can understand from hindsight that German fascism was a product of these ideas and a child of its times.

Iqbal summed up his reaction to this European civilization in :

तुम्हारी तहज़ीब अपनी खंजर से आप ही खुदकुशी करेगी
जो शाख़े नाज़ुक पे आशियाना बनेगा नापायदार होगा

Your civilization will commit suicide with its own sword
The nest built on delicate bough is bound to fall

and in his chastisement :

दयार-ए मग़रिब के रहने वालो खुदा की बस्ती दुकां नहीं है

You, the people of the west, God's worship is not a
matter of profit and loss

The Controversial Iqbal

Iqbal has been quite controversial especially among the non-Muslims of the sub-continent. It is contended that from a great nationalist poet, he turned pro-Islamic, sectarian, even communal. The genesis of Pakistan is attributed to him. It is undoubtedly true that it was he who first conceived the idea of a separate Muslim state and wrote long letters to Mohammed Ali Jinnah to give it a practical shape. "The enforcement and development of Shariat," he had written," is impossible in this country without a free Muslim state or states." Again, in 1937, appealing to Jinnah to take up the cause of Pakistan he wrote, "Why shouldn't the Muslims of North-West India and Bengal be considered a nation entitled to self determination…." In a foreword to Iqbal's 'Letters' in 1943, Jinnah acknowledged Iqbal's contribution to the creation of Pakistan, "Sir Mohammed played a very conspicuous part in bringing about the consummation." Iqbal himself admitted to *The Times*, London that there was a need for a separate federation of Muslim provinces, and he told Dickinson, who had translated his Persian poems, that his ideal society was Muslim society. However, it was his presidential address at the Allahabad session of the Muslim League, in 1930, which alienated many of his non-Muslim admirers.

While all this is very true, Iqbal cannot be called a communalist. For one thing, he never preached hatred towards Hindus (or any other religion), which for all his secularism, Jinnah did not refrain from. On the contrary, in poems like 'Naya Shivala' (The New Temple), it was Hindu-Muslim unity, which he championed most effectively. He wrote poems, on India's past grandeur and glory and eulogized the great Indians belonging to all religions. If we have poems on Daagh, Shibli and Haali, there are celebratory pieces on Swami Ram Tirath, Nanak and Ram too. In his youth, Iqbal's patriotic fervour was at its peak. It was in this period that he composed some of his most popular lyrics like *Tarana-e-Hind.* (The Song of India). Lala Hardayal, a great patriot who was exiled by the British, had formed a club in Lahore, called Young Men's Indian Association. He was a close friend of Iqbal, who was at that time at the peak of his fame. Hardayal invited Iqbal to inaugurate the new club. On this occasion, instead of delivering a formal lecture, Iqbal recited *Tarana-e-Hind*. The poem cast a spell on the gathering. As he read one couplet after the other, the audience went into raptures. No less a man than Mahatma Gandhi said of the 'Tarana', "Which Indian heart will not throb on hearing Iqbal's 'Hindustan Hamara'. Is the language of the song Hindi or Urdu? Who will say this is not the natural language of India? I am quite clear that neither Sanskritised Hindi nor Persianised Urdu will win the race, Hindustani will". Iqbal was much troubled by the growing disunity among Hindus and Muslims, intensified by the Hindi-Urdu controversy. It was in this mood that in 'Naya Shivala', Iqbal made a powerful plea to both Hindus and Muslims to get rid of their worn out ideas and give up mutual distrust and ill-will. This poem too, like the 'Tarana', won acclaim from Indians across the spectrum. Similarly, one of the earliest poems that Iqbal wrote is 'Himalaya', which remains unsurpassed in describing the majesty and grandeur of this sentinel of India.

In his Persian poem *Javed Nama* which is regarded as Iqbal's magnum opus and a counterpart of Dante's *Divine Comedy*, the poet visits various stellar spheres and meets many historical and spiritual personalities and elucidates some eternal truths. Rumi accompanies him, like Dante is accompanied by Virgil. One of the persons they meet there is a Kashmiri Persian poet, Ghani, in conversation with whom Iqbal makes an obvious reference to the contribution of Nehru family in the freedom struggle :

The lovely scion of a Brahmin family,
The red tulip feels shy before their ruddy faces
Farsighted, experienced and hardy they are
Their origin is from our land.

And when leaders like Moti Lal Nehru and Gandhi were jailed, Iqbal wrote :

The crows and the vultures are never encaged
The honour goes to the hawks and the falcons only

On the celebrations of victory in the First World War, when all participants got their share, India, Iqbal sarcastically remarked, was allotted only the 'name of God'.

The poem on Swami Ram Tirath is full of Indian philosophical sentiment, and immediately after the 'Tarana', Iqbal translated the 'Gayatri Mantra' into Urdu and prefaced it with a long explanation approaching it from the Islamic point of view. Similarly, in 'The Song of the Indian Children', he extols the teachings of Nanak and Chishti. In *Bang-e-Dra*, his first Urdu collection (1924), Iqbal comes across as a supremely nationalist poet.

It is his later poetry that raised the hackles of many. It is regretted that such a great poet of the whole of Hindustan should increasingly and exclusively become a poet of Islam. The fact of the matter, however, is that he was much moved by the plight of the Muslims—their ignorance, their inertia, low self-esteem, poverty and their habit of living in past glory—and felt a powerful urge to lift them from the stupor into which they had fallen.

Developments at home and abroad also contributed to his shift towards Islam. For one, he concluded that the differences between Hindus and Muslims were becoming irreconciliable and a separate federation of Muslim provinces was the only way in which they could secure peaceful India and save the Muslims from the domination of the non-Muslims. Externally, the Ottoman Sultan, the Caliph of Islam was facing a revolt from his Christian subjects in Balkans. The Caliph was the guardian of Mecca and Madina and challenge to his authority was considered by Muslims as a challenge to Islam. Iqbal too was disturbed because he feared that the West was bent upon destroying Islam. Holding the *Quran* in his hand, Gladstone, the British prime minister had declared in the House of Commons, "So long as there is this book, there will be no peace in the world." This could be quite scary.

While it is not wrong to say that Iqbal was a poet of Islam, his appeal like the appeal of Christian Milton and Hindu Kalidas was universal, says Sir Tej Bahadur Sapru. Iqbal's Islam was pan-Islamic. He wanted to reform and rejuvenate Islam and he was very critical of Mullas and Maulvis:

जंगो-जदल सिखाया वाइज़ को भी खुदा ने

To the Mullah also, God has only the path of battle shown

And the Pakistan that was finally created does not conform to his concept of the Islamic state. It was the non-terrestrial state that he sang of. In this connection, Rafiq Zakaria has sketched a telling contrast between Iqbal and Jinnah. Jinnah was cold, calculating, indifferent to others; he was successful as a lawyer and a politician, his outlook was western and he was not grounded in Islam, inspite of his advocacy of Pakistan. Iqbal, on the other hand, was warm, generous, friendly but a failure both as a lawyer and a politician. He did not separate politics from religion and lived and worked for Islamic renaissance, whereas Jinnah was secular. When Nehru met Iqbal, the poet himself remarked, "What is common between you and Jinnah. He is a politician, you are a patriot." A great tribute to Jawaharlal, indeed.

And although Iqbal writes about Islam, he writes with such passion and intensity that his poetry becomes a source of inspiration for all humanity. As Mian Bashir Ahmed says, though Iqbal frequently addressed himself to the Muslims, he spoke so forcefully, so truly that it becomes a call to all mankind. In fact, his ideal Muslim is an ideal man. Spiritual teachings of the East and the dynamism of the West coexist in Iqbal. He had drunk deep on the fountains of Eastern and Western thought, and as his talent gathered form, depth, beauty and majesty, his writing became a vehicle for humanistic urges. In this sense, he is a secular poet. According to Sarojini Naidu, Iqbal's best poetry is essentially human and touching; it strikes a deep chord in man's heart and mind.

Although Iqbal is a poet with a message and a man with a mission, his poetry never degenerates into propaganda. In fact, the reason why this poetry has a mighty pull is because it is great poetry judged on the highest artistic standards. There is a loftiness, a sweep, a finesse and beauty that elicits instant admiration. It is a poetry that grows in the breast of the poet, and hence it is genuine poetry. It is a poetry that is god-given and hence spontaneous. As Maulvi Abdul Haq says, Iqbal's poetry breathes sincerity. Some of his longer poems like 'Khizr-e-Rah', 'Shama Aur Shair', 'Masjid-e-Qarteba' and 'Walide Murhooma Ki Yaad Main', dealing with lofty themes, bring to our mind the grandeur of Milton. They carry the full soul-force of the poet. According to A.J. Arbery, both Milton and Iqbal are poet prophets.

Iqbal's stay in Europe was a watershed in the growth and

development of his mind. Back home in 1908, he occupied himself with the quest for a remedy for the weaknesses of his people. He was greatly perturbed by the backwardness, inertia and poverty in which the Muslims were trapped. Now on, it became a mission with him to retrieve them from this quagmire. And hence, the pro-Islamic character that his writing took.

Iqbal's reputation as a poet of international stature was established with the publication of 'Asrar-e-Khudi' (Secrets of the Self) in Persian. Some other poems in Persian followed and, in recognition of his contribution to world literature, Allahabad University conferred on him the degree of Doctor of Literature.

After his return from Europe, when Iqbal was writing mainly in Persian, his friends and admirers impressed upon him the need for writing in Urdu, a language which was understood by large masses. He was persuaded and his first collection of Urdu poetry, *Bang-e-Dara* (The Call of the Caravan) appeared in 1924. This book is perhaps the best that Iqbal wrote and his reputation as a great poet at least in India, rests on it. The book has three parts. Part I contains the poems which he composed before he left for Europe in 1905. Part II contains poems which he wrote during his stay in Europe and Part III contains the poems after he returned from Europe. *Bang-e-Dara* was followed by *Bal-e-Jibreel* in 1935, and *Zarb-e-Kalim* in 1938 published after Iqbal's death. His fourth book is Armughane Hujaj.

Being a champion of his community's cause, Iqbal could not stay away long from party politics, though his heart was not at all in it. After the First World War, new and revolutionary ideas were creating a ferment in the Islamic world. For one, there was the Khilafat movement, which was supported by both Hindus and Muslims in India. In 1927, Iqbal was elected to the Punjab Legislative Council. He was also the Secretary of All India Muslim League, a position from which he resigned in 1929 because of his differences of opinion, especially on the question of provincial autonomy. Earlier, in 1922, the British Crown conferred Knighthood upon him. Some critics have rightly maintained that the acceptance of the knighthood was not compatible with Iqbal's staunch opposition to the British rule and the lofty ideals he had preached. In fact, though much affected by the plight of the Muslims, he never participated in any agitation against the British. As Rafiq Zakaria says, Iqbal was a rebel only in poetry, not in action; he was an arm-chair politician.

In 1930, Iqbal presided over the Allahabad session of All India Muslim League, where his presidential address electrified the Muslims and dismayed his Hindu admirers. In this address, for the first time, he put forth the idea of a separate homeland for the Muslims. He said that Punjab, North-West Frontier Province, Sindh and Baluchistan be amalgamated into a single state and added that self-government within or without the British Empire was the final destiny of the Muslims of North-West India. In this address lay the seeds of Pakistan. Yet at that time, as Indian nationalism was at its zenith, nobody took Iqbal seriously. The Congress Party was the dominating political force and Muslim League was considered a party of reactionaries, who were interested in safeguarding the interests of the feudal elements and who wanted to perpetuate their hold on the ignorant and illiterate Muslim masses.

In the last month of 1931, Iqbal attended the Second Round Table Conference in London as a member of the All India Muslim delegation. The idea of a separate homeland for the Muslims was mooted in this conference also, but it found few takers. Iqbal was dubbed by some people as a reactionary who was out of sync with the modern times. He fell out of favour with the leader of the Muslim delegation, Sir Akbar Hydari. On his way back, Iqbal attended the World Muslim Congress in Jerusalem. In the autumn of 1932, he went back to London to attend the Third Round Table Conference. After the conference, he reached Paris where he met Bergson, whose philosophy had influenced him in youth. He visited Spain and from there he went to Italy. He met Mussolini and wrote a poem in which he saw a saint and devil combined in him.

Iqbal had settled permanently in Lahore after his return from

Europe. For some time he worked as a teacher in a college but soon resigned and started his legal practice. He did not do well as a lawyer, for, he was more interested in philosophy and literature than law. Financially, he was not too well off. The last years of his life were rendered more difficult by financial troubles because the treatment for his various ailments was quite expensive. He suffered from a very sore throat, which could not be cured despite the best treatment. Otherwise also, he kept very bad health in those years and became a recluse. He said what difference does it make if one lives a little longer? Why then take the trouble of exercise and medicine?

In May 1935, his eyes developed cataract and he was almost completely deprived from reading and writing. Then, he developed problem in his kidney and his breathlessness increased too. One day, without telling anybody, he prepared his Will. He was treated by two Unani hakeems who came specially from Delhi, but to no avail. The worst came when he started vomiting blood and the voice that moved masses in the country and outside was stilled on April 21, 1938. As the news of his death spread, people from all walks of life started gathering at Javed Manzil, where at that time he lived in Lahore. An estimated eight thousand people joined the funeral procession. Shops and establishments were closed in Lahore and many other towns. Condolence meetings were held in which rare tributes were paid to the great poet. A number of prominent people, including Tagore, sent condolences. "India whose place in the world is too narrow" said Tagore, "can ill afford to miss a poet whose poetry had such universal value."

This poet who captivated vast audiences with the magical cadence, musical ecstasy and the soul-stirring message of his poetry, however, got less than his due in his lifetime. The people who were to benefit by using his name after his death, did not care much for him when he was alive. He lacked tact, which is so essential for winning friends and influencing people. In fact, he would annoy people in position who could help him. All said and done, he was a very simple man, leading an austere life.

In spite of being Knighted, he was extremely unassuming. He did hanker after more luscious prizes and preferments and made compromises. But, whenever he stooped to conquer, he made the worst of both the worlds. Like most genuinely creative artists, he could not manipulate people. Although his 'Asrar-e-Khudi' (Secrets of the Self) in Persian created a stir in the dovecotes of pseudo mystics, for the Iranians, he was only "a local poet" and in the West his reputation was hindered because of the difficulties of translation. He met Bergson in Paris, but in London no English thinker or writer took note of him when he went there to attend the Round Table Conference. As Iqbal Singh says, while he was sure of his ultimate worth, he wanted Western recognition and tangible rewards, the absence of which gave him a gnawing sense of grievance and bitterness. "My rivals have carried on a propaganda against me…to prejudice the men in authority…In this, they have succeeded so far," he wrote. In India, his reputation has suffered because of his role in the creation of Pakistan.

Be it as it may, however, those who have read and enjoyed Iqbal would vouch that no poet in the sub-continent and perhaps the whole of Asia has left behind such valuable treasure as Iqbal has :

हज़ारों साल नरगिस अपनी बेनूरी पे रोती है
बड़ी मुश्किल से होता है चमन में दीदावर पैदा

For ages, Narcissus bewails its purblind state
The birth of a discerning mind is an event rare and great.

Faiz Ahmed Faiz, who was such a great poet himself, wittily said after Iqbal's death, "It is good that Iqbal turned towards religion. If he had turned to the writing of ghazals with the same passion, poets like me would have been nowhere."

–Kuldip Salil

Contents

Ghazals & Nazms

गेसू-ए-ताबदार[1] को और भी ताबदार कर
होश-ओ ख़िरद[2] शिकार कर, क़ल्ब-ओ-नज़र[3] शिकार कर

तू है मुहीत-ए-बेकराँ[4], मैं हूँ ज़रा सी आबजू[5]
या मुझे हमकिनार[6] कर, या मुझे बेकिनार[7] कर

मैं हूँ सदफ़[8] तो तेरे हाथ मेरे गुहर की आबरू
मैं हूँ खज़फ[9] तो तू मुझे गौहर-ए-आबदार कर

बाग़-ए-बिहिश्त[10] से मुझे हुक्म-ए-सफ़र दिया था क्यूँ
कार-ए-जहाँ[11] दराज़ है, अब मेरा इंतिज़ार कर

रोज़-ए-हिसाब जब मेरा पेश हो दफ़्तर-ए-अमल
आप भी शर्मसार हो, मुझको भी शर्मसार कर

Gesu-e-taabdaar ko aur bhi taabdaar kar
hosh-o-khird shikar kar, qalb-o-nazar shikar kar

Tu hai muhit-e-bekaran, main hoon zara si aabju
Ya mujhe humkinar kar, ya mujhe bekinar kar

Main hoon sadaf to tere hath mere gauhar ki aabru
main hoon khazaf to tu mujhe gauhar-e-aabdaar kar

Bagh-e-bihisht se mujhe hukm-e-safar diya tha kyun
Kaar-e-jahan daraz hai, ab mira intizaar kar

Roz-e-hisab jab mera pesh ho daftar-e-amal
Aap bhi sharmsar ho, mujkko bhi sharmsar kar

---

1. चमकती लटें 2. बुद्धि और चेतना 3. हृदय और दृष्टि 4. असीम 5. नदी 6. बगलगीर 7. व्यापक 8. सीपी 9. ठीकरा 10. स्वर्ग 11. संसार का काम

Let your shining hair still brighter shine
Enthrall my sense and reason, my eye and this
heart of mine

Thou art an ocean limitless, and I a little stream only
Either absorb me, or make me boundless like thee

If I am a shell, it is upto you, whether or not I
hold a pearl
If I am a pebble, make a pearl out of the pebble

Why did you turn me out of the Garden of
Eden, in the first place
There is much work to do on earth still, so let
you wait now, your grace!

On the Day of Judgement, when the angels
present my balance sheet
Let you also feel ashamed, O God, as you make
me feel the heat

तेरे इश्क़ की इन्तिहा चाहता हूँ
मेरी सादगी देख क्या चाहता हूँ

सितम[1] हो कि हो वादा-ए-बेहिजाबी[2]
कोई बात सब्र-आज़मा[3] चाहता हूँ

यह जन्नत मुबारक रहे ज़ाहिदों[4] को
कि मैं आपका सामना चाहता हूँ

भरी बज़्म में राज़ की बात कह दी
बड़ा बेअदब हूँ, सज़ा चाहता हूँ

कोई दम का मेहमाँ हूँ ऐ अहले-महफ़िल
चिराग़े-सहर[5] हूँ बुझा चाहता हूँ

Tere ishq ki intiha chahta hoon
Meri saadgi dekh kya chahta hoon

Sitam ho ki ho vada-e-behijabi
koi baat sabr-aazma chahta hoon

Yeh jannat mubarak rahe zahidon ko
ki main aapka saamna chahta hoon

Koi dam ka mehman hun ae ahle-mehfil
Chirag-e-sehar hun bujha chahta hoon

Bhari bazm mein raaz ki baat keh di
Bara beadab hun, saza chahta hoon

---

1. अत्याचार 2. पर्दा हटाने का वादा 3. धैर्य को आज़माने वाली 4. संयमियों 5. सुबह का दीपक

I want your love to cross every limit
Look at my simplicity, look at it

Be it cruelty or your unveiled beauty
I want something to test me to extremity

Let the preacher find heavenly grace
I want to see you face to face

In full assembly I have revealed your secret
I lack all manners, I must be punished for it

Like the morning candle whose light with the dawn ends
Only a little while in the gathering, I'll be with you now, O my friends

अनोखी वज़अ[1] है सारे ज़माने से निराले हैं
ये आशिक़ कौन-सी बस्ती के या रब रहने वाले हैं

इलाजे-दर्द में भी दर्द की लज़्ज़त पे मरता हूँ
जो थे छालों में काँटे नोके-सोज़न[2] से निकाले हैं

फला-फूला रहे या रब चमन मेरी उमीदों का
जिगर का खून दे-देकर ये बूटे मैंने पाले हैं

न पूछो मुझसे लज़्ज़त ख़ानुमाँ-बरबाद[3] रहने की
नशेमन[4] सैकड़ों मैंने बनाकर फूँक डाले हैं

उमीदे-ए-हूर ने सब कुछ सिखा रखा है वाइज़ को
ये हज़रत देखने में सीधे-सादे भोले-भाले हैं

नहीं बेगानगी अच्छी रफ़ीक़े-राहे-मंज़िल[5] से
ठहर जा ऐ शरर[6]! हम भी तो आख़िर मिटने वाले हैं

Anokhi wazá hai saare zamane se nirale hain
Ye aashiq kaun-si basti ke ya Rab rehne wale hain

Ilaj-e-dard mein bhi dard ki lazzat pe marta hoon
Jo the chhalon mein kante noke-soza se nikale hain

Foola-Foola rahe yaarub chaman meri umidon ka
Jigar ka khoon de-dekar ye boote maine paale hain

Na puchho mujhse lazzat khanuma-barbaad rehne ki
Nasheman sainkron maine banakar phoonk daale hain

Umid-e-hoor ne sab kuchh sikha rakha hai vaiz ko
Ye hazrat dekhne mein sidhe-saade bhole-bhale hain

Nahin begangi achchi rafiqe-raahe-manzil se
Thehar ja ae sharar, hum bhi to aakhir mitne wale hain

---

1. रंग-ढंग 2. सूई की नोक 3. नष्ट हो चुके घर में 4. घोंसला 5. सहयात्री 6. चिंगारी

A class apart in manner and mould, unique and odd
To which country do these lovers belong,
O dear God

I relish the pain even though this pain I seek to treat
With a twisted pin I remove the thorn from my feet

These blossoms of my hope, O Lord, may they
always flourish
For them, I have given my lifeblood in order to
nourish

The joy of living in a ruined abode, O ask me not
A thousand nests I have built and to cinders wrought

The hope of getting the hoors in heaven has taught
him everything
By design only, the preacher is innocent-looking

It is not proper to behave stranger-like to a fellow
traveller, O friend
Wait a bit, O spark, for I too am hastening towards
my end

सितारों से आगे जहाँ और भी हैं
अभी इश्क़ के इम्तिहाँ और भी हैं

क़नाअत[1] न कर आलम[2]-ए-रंग-ओ-बू पर
चमन और भी, आशियाँ और भी हैं

अगर खो गया इक नशेमन तो क्या ग़म
मक़ामात-ए-आह-ओ फ़ुग़ाँ[3] और भी हैं

तू शाहीं[4] है परवाज़[5] है काम तेरा
तिरे सामने आसमाँ और भी हैं

इसी रोज़-ओ-शब में उलझ कर न रह जा
कि तेरे ज़मान-ओ-मक़ाँ[6] और भी हैं

गए दिन कि तन्हा था मैं अंजुमन में
यहाँ अब मिरे राज़दाँ और भी हैं

Sitaron se aage jahan aur bhi hain
Abhi ishq ke imtihan aur bhi hain

Qanát na kar aalam-e-rang-o-bu per
Chaman aur bhi, aashiyan aur bhi hain

Agar kho gaya ik nasheman to kya ghum
Maqamaat-e-aah-o fugan aur bhi hain

Tu shahin hai parvaaz hai kaam tera
Tire samne aasman aur bhi hain

Isee roz-o-shab mein ulajh kar na reh jaa
Ki tere zamaan-o-makan aur bhi hain

Gaye din ki tanha tha main anjuman mein
Yahan ab mire raazdan aur bhi hain

---

1. संतोष 2 संसार 3. आर्तनाद 4. बाज़ 5. उड़ान 6. देश-काल

There are worlds beyond the stars too
And many more trials in love still to go through

Do not stop at this world of fragrance and colour
There are abodes still more, many more gardens,
dear

What if that one abode you no longer keep
There are other places for you to sigh and weep

You are an eagle, your job is higher, and higher
to fly
There are before you to climb, still many a sky

Within the space of day and night do not remain
confined
There are more space and times for you still to find

Gone are the days when I was alone in the assembly
I have now here, my confidants in plenty

ज़माना देखेगा जब मेरे दिल से महशर[1] उठेगा गुफ़्तगू का
मेरी ख़ामोशी नहीं है, गोया मज़ार[2] है हर्फ़े-आरज़ू[3] का

जो मौज-ए-दरिया लगी यह कहने सफ़र से क़ायम है शान मेरी
गुहर[4] यह बोला सदफ़-नशीनी[5] है मुझको सामान आबरू का

कोई दिल ऐसा नज़र न आया, न जिसमें ख़्वाबीदा[6] हो तमन्ना
इलाही तेरा जहान क्या है, निगारख़ाना है आरज़ू का

अगर कोई शै नहीं है पिनहां तो क्यों सरापा तलाश हूँ मैं
निगह को नज़ारे की तमन्ना है, दिल को सौदा है जुस्तजू का

न हो तबीयत ही जिनकी क़ाबिल वो तरबियत में नहीं सँवरते
हुआ न सरसब्ज़ रहके पानी में अक्स-सर्व-ए-किनारे-जू[7] का

Zamana dekhega jab mere dil se mehshar uthega guftgu ka
Meri khamoshi nahin hai, goya mazaar hai harph-e-aarzu ka

Jo mauj-e-dariya lagi yeh kehne safar se qayam hai shaan meri
Guhar yeh bola sadaf-nashini hai mujhko samaan aabru ka

Koi dil aisa nazar na aaya, na jismein khwabida ho tamanna
Ilahi tera jahan kya hai, nigarkhana hai aarzu ka

Agar koi shai nahin hai pinhan to kyon sarapa talash hun main
Nigah ko nazzare ki tamanna hai, dil ko sauda hai justjoo ka

Na ho tabiyat hi jinki qabil voh tarbiyat mein nahin sanwarte
Hua na sarsabz rehke paani mein akse-saru-e-kinare-zoo ka

---

1. प्रलय 2. क़ब्र 3. इच्छाएं 4. मोती 5. सीपी में रहना 6. सोई हुई 7. नदी किनारे के पेड़ों की परछाईं

The world would see when my heart speaks up
like a blast
My silence is not silence, it is a grave of my desires
first and last

As the wave in the river averred, "My glory lies in
travel eternal"
"In residing in the shell lies my dignity", said the
pearl

Not a heart, which is not a house of desire,
have I seen
What is this world O Lord, but a gallery of longings
sharp and keen

The heart yearns for fulfilment, the eye is longing
for the sight,
What is it that I am looking for day and night

If there is no aptitude, education will hardly
anything mean
The shadow of the tree on the river bank will never
become green.

फ़िर चराग़-ए-लाला से रोशन हुए कोह-ओ-दमन
फ़िर मुझे नग़मों पे उकसाने लगा मुर्ग़-ए-चमन

फूल हैं सहरा में या परियाँ क़तार-अन्दर-क़तार
ऊदे-ऊदे, नीले-नीले, पीले-पीले पैरहन

बर्ग-ए-गुल पे रख गयी शबनम का मोती बाद-ए-सुबह
और चमकाती है उस मोती को सूरज की किरन

अपने मन में डूबकर पा जा सुराग़-ए-ज़िन्दगी
तू अगर मेरा नहीं बनता न बन, अपना तो बन

Phir charag-e-laala se roshan hue koh-o-daman
phir mujhe naghmon pe uksane laga murghe-chaman

Phool hain sehra mein ya pariyan kataar-ander-kataar
ude-ude, neele-neele, peele-peele perhan

Barg-e-gul pe rakh gayee shabnam ka moti bade-subah
aur chamkati hai us moti ko suraj ki kiran

Apne man mein doobkar paa jaa surag-e-zindgi
tu agar mera nahin banta na ban, apna to ban

→

Again the hill and the valley are with the light of tulips lit
Once again the garden-bird incites me into a lyrical fit

Apparalled in robes, pink, blue and yellow
The flowers in the garden look like fairies row within row

The morning breeze has left pearl-like dew on the rose-petal
And the ray of the sun makes that pearl glitter

By delving deep into your own soul, the secret of life, find
Be at least your own, if you don't want to become mine

→

मन की दौलत हाथ आती है तो फिर जाती नहीं
तन की दौलत छाँव है, आता है धन, जाता है धन

मन की दुनिया में न पाया मैंने अफरंगी का राज़
मन की दुनिया में न देखे मैंने शेख़ो-बिरहमन

पानी-पानी कर गयी मुझको क़लंदर की ये बात
तू झुका जब ग़ैर के आगे, न मन तेरा न तन

Man ki daulat haath aati hai to phir jaati nahin
tan ki daulat chhaon hai aata hai dhan, jaata hai dhan

Man ki duniyan mein na paaya maine afrangi ka raaj
man ki duniyan mein na dekhe maine shekho-brahman

Paani-paani kar gayee mujhko qalandar ki ye baat
tu jhuka jab ghair ke aage, na man tera na tan

Once you acquire inner wealth, it is never lost
Material possessions are shadows which come and go past

In the inner world, no alien rule I find
There is neither the Sheikh nor the Brahmin in the world of the mind

The moment you yield to the enemy, neither the mind is yours, nor the body
These words of the hermit shamed me immensely

मजनूं ने शहर छोड़ा तू सेहरा भी छोड़ दे
नज़्ज़ारे की हवस है तो लैला भी छोड़ दे

वाइज़! कमाल-ए-तर्क से मिलती है यां मुराद
दुनिया जो छोड़ दी है तो उक़बा[1] भी छोड़ दे

है आशिक़ी में रस्म अलग सबसे बैठना
बुतख़ाना भी, हरम भी, कलीसा भी छोड़ दे

सौदागरी नहीं, यह इबादत ख़ुदा की है
ऐ बेख़बर, जज़ा[2] की तमन्ना भी छोड़ दे

अच्छा है दिल के साथ रहे पासबाने-अक़्ल[3]
लेकिन कभी-कभी इसे तनहा भी छोड़ दे

Majnoon ne shehar chhora to sehra bhi chhor de
nazzare ki hawas hai to Laila bhi chhor de

Waiz ! kamal-e-tark se milti hai yaan murad
duniya jo chhor di hai to uqba bhi chhor de

Hai aashiqi mein rasm alag sabse baithna
butkhana bhi, haram bhi, kalisa bhi chhor de

Saudagri nahin, yeh ibadat khuda ki hai
ae bekhabar, jazaa ki tamanna bhi chhor de

Achha hai dil ke saath rahe paasban-e-aql
lekin kabhi-kabhi ise tanha bhi chhor de

1. परलोक 2. प्रतिफल 3. बुद्धिरूपी रक्षक

Majnu left the town, let you leave the desert too
If you are desirous of her sight, let you forget
Laila too

By giving up everything you win the boon, O preacher!
If you have renounced this world, think not of
heaven either

The lovers as a rule should go their lonely way
Away from the temple and the church, as also from
the Kaba should you stay

It is God's worship, and not a business
O you ignorant one, think not of the reward in this

Good, if the heart is accompanied by the mind
But sometime, let it also its own company find

कभी ऐ हक़ीक़ते-मुन्तज़र[1] नज़र आ लिबासे-मजाज़[2] में।
कि हज़ारों सिजदे तड़प रहे हैं मेरी जबीन-ए-नियाज़[3] में

तू बचा-बचा के न रख इसे, तेरा आईना है वो आईना
कि शिकस्ता[4] हो तो अज़ीज़तर है निगाह-ए-आईनासाज़[5] में

न कहीं जहां में अमां[6] मिली जो अमां मिली तो कहां मिली
मेरे ज़ुर्म-ए-ख़ाना-ख़राब को तेरे अफ़ु-ए-बन्दा-नवाज़[7] में

न वो इश्क़ में रहीं गर्मियां न वो हुस्न में रहीं शोख़ियां
न वो ग़ज़नवी में तड़प रही न वो ख़म है ज़ुल्फ़-ए-अयाज़[8] में

जो मैं सर-ब-सिजदा हुआ कभी तो ज़मीं से आने लगी सदा
तेरा दिल तो है सनम-आशना तुझे क्या मिलेगा नमाज़ में

Kabhi ae haqiqat-e-muntzar nazar aa libas-e-majaz mein
Ki hazaron sijde tarap rahe hain meri jabin-e-niyaaz mein

Tu bacha-bacha ke na rakh ise, tera aaina hai woha-aina
Ki shikasta ho to aziztar hai nigaahe-aainasaaz mein

Na kahin jahan mein amaan mili, jo amman mili to kahan mili
Mere jurm-e-khana-kharab ko tere afu-banda-nawaz mein

Na woh ishq mein rahin garmiyan ne woh husn mein rahin shokhiyan
Na woh ghazanvi mein tarap rahi na woh kham hai zulfe-ayaz mein

Jo main sar-b-sijda hua kabhi to zamin se aane lagi sada
Tera dil to hai sanam-aashna tujhe kya milega namaz mein

---

1. प्रतीक्षित ईश्वरीय प्रेम 2. सांसारिक प्रेम के लिबास में 3. प्रेमी का माथा 4. टूट जाए 5. आईना बनाने वाले की नज़र में 6. पनाह 7. क्षमाशीलता तथा कृपा 8. ग़ज़नवी का प्रिय दास

O long awaited divine love, manifest sometime
in worldly form too
My forehead is fervently longing to rub itself
before you

Don't be too protective towards it, for such is
your mirror
That if it breaks, it' ll be lovelier in the eyes of
its maker

Nowhere could my crime at large, a sanctuary find
If ultimately it did, it was in your forgiveness kind

Neither do we find that warmth in love, nor that
glitter in beauty
Neither has Ghaznavi that burning passion, nor his
slave Ayyaz's hair curly

Whenever I bend in prayer, a voice from the earth
I begin to hear:
Your heart is longing for worldly love, what'll you
gain out of the prayer?

लाऊँ वह तिनके कहां से आशियाने के लिए,
बिजलियाँ बेताब हों जिनको जलाने के लिए

वाय नाकामी! फ़लक ने ताक कर तोड़ा उसे,
मैंने जिस डाली को ताड़ा आशियाने के लिए

दिल में कोई इस तरह की आरज़ू पैदा करूँ,
लौट जाय आस्माँ मेरे मिटाने के लिए

पास था नाकामी-ए-सैयाद का ऐ हमसफ़र
वर्ना मैं, और उड़ के आता एक दाने के लिए।

इस चमन में मुर्ग-ए-दिल गाये न आज़ादी का गीत,
आह! यह गुलशन नहीं ऐसे तराने के लिए

laaun woh tinke kahan se aashiyane ke liye
bijliyan betaab hon jinko jalane ke liye

Vaye nakami ! Falak ne taak kar tora use
maine jis daali ko tara aashiyane ke liye

Dil mein koi is tarah ki aarzu paida karoon
laut jaaye aasman mere mitane ke liye

Paas tha nakami-e-saiyaad ka ae humsafar
Warna main, aur ur ke aata ek daane ke liye

Is chaman mein murg-e-dil gaaye ne azadi ka geet
aah ! yeh gulshan nahin aise tarane ke liye

From where shall I get the straws for my nest
That the lightning, until it burns them, would
not rest

Misery, that heaven should especially break
The twig on which I had decided my nest to make

I wish I were fired by such a passion
That to thwart it should be the heaven's mission

It is for the sake of the hunter that I chose
to descend
Otherwise, for a grain of corn, do you think I
would bend?

O heart, sing not the song of freedom here
This garden is not meant for such a fare

फिर बाद-ए-बहार[1] आई, 'इक़बाल' .गज़लख्वां[2] हो
गुंचा है अगर गुल हो, गुल हो तो गुलिस्तां हो

तू ख़ाक. की मुट्ठी है, अजज़ा[3] की हरारत से
बरहम हो, परेशां हो, वुसअत[4] में बयाबां हो

तू जिन्स-ए-मोहब्बत है क़ीमत है गिरां[5] तेरी
कम-माया हैं सौदागर इस देश में अर्ज़ां[6] हो

सामां की मोहब्बत में मुज़मिर है[7] तन-आसानी।
मक़सद है अगर मंज़िल, .गारतगरे-सामां[8] हो॥

Phir bad-e-bahaar aai, 'Iqbal' gazalkhwan ho
Guncha hai agar gul ho, gul ho to gulistan ho

Tu khaaq ki mutthi hai, ajzaa ki hararat se
Barhum ho, pareshan ho, vusát main bayaban ho

Tu jins-e-mohabbat hai qimat hai giran teri
Kam-maaya hain saudagar is desh mein arzaan ho

Saaman ki mohabbat mein muzmir hai tan-asaani
Maqsad hai agar manzil, gharatgare-samaan ho

---

1. वसंत ऋतु की हवा 2. गीत गाओ 3. तत्त्वों 4. फैलाव 5. महँगी 6. रास्ता 7. निहित 8. सामान को नष्ट करने वाला

The spring breezes blow, so Iqbal, go singing
If a bud you are, be a blossom, if blossom, a garden in spring

With the heat of elements, O you who are only a handful of dust
Let you stir and expand and become a vast desert

You are love incarnate, a precious commodity
The traders here lack capital, so leave this country

The love of material goods makes you ease loving
If destination is your motive, forego every other thing

गुलज़ार-ए-हस्तो-बूद[1] न बेगानावार[2] देख
है देखने की चीज़ इसे बार-बार देख

आया है तू जहां में मिसाल-ए-शरार[3] देख
दम दे न जाए हस्ती-ए-नापायदारा[4] देख

माना कि तेरे दीद के क़ाबिल नहीं हूं मैं
तू मेरा शौक़ देख, मेरा इन्तज़ार देख

Gulzar-e-hasto-bood na beganawar dekh
hai dekhne ki cheez ise baar-baar dekh

Aaya hai tu jahan mein misale-sharar dekh
dum de na jaaye hasti-e-napayedaar dekh

Maana ki tere deed ke qabil nahin hoon main
tu mera shauq dekh, mera intzaar dekh

---

1. संसार को 2. उदासीन दृष्टि से 3. चिंगारी की तरह 4. नश्वर जीवन

See it not like a stranger; do not in the garden of
life an alien remain
It is a thing worth seeing, see it again and again

You have come into the world like a spark, you
should know
Watch out lest this life should unrequited go

I am not worthy of you, I concede
But see my patience, the love in my eyes you
should read

जिन्हें मैं ढूँढ़ता था आस्मानों में ज़मीनों में
वो निकले मेरे ज़ुलमत-ख़ाना-ए-दिल[1] के मकीनों में

महीने वस्ल के घड़ियों की सूरत उड़ते जाते हैं
मगर घड़ियां जुदाई की गुज़रती हैं महीनों में

तमन्ना दर्द-ए-दिल की हो तो कर ख़िदमत फ़क़ीरों की
नहीं मिलता यह गौहर बादशाहों के ख़ज़ीनों में

मुहब्बत के लिए दिल ढूँढ़ कोई टूटने वाला
यह वो मय है जिसे रखते हैं नाज़ुक आबगीनों[2] में

ख़मोश ऐ दिल! भरी महफिल में चिल्लाना नहीं अच्छा
अदब पहला क़रीना है मुहब्बत के क़रीनों में

बुरा समझूं उन्हें, मुझ से तो ऐसा हो नहीं सकता
कि मैं खुद भी तो हूँ इक़बाल अपने नुक्ताचीनों में

Jinhen main dhoondhta tha aasmanon mein zaminon mein
woh nikle mere zulmat-khana-e-dil ke makinon mein

Mahine vasl ke ghariyon ki surat urte jaate hain
magar ghariyan judai ki guzarti han mahinon mein

Tamanna dardie-dil ki ho to kar khidmat phakiri ki
nahin milta yeh gauhar baadshahon ke khazinon mein

Muhabbat ke liye dil dhoondh koi tootne wala
yeh veh mai hai jise rakhte hain nazuk aabgino mein

Khamosh ae dil ! bhari mehfil mein chillana nahin achha
adab pehla qarina hai muhabbat qe karino mein

Bura samjhoon unhen, mujhse to aisa ho nahin sakta
Ki main khud bhi to hoon Iqbal apne nuktacheenon mein

1. दिल का अंधेरा घर 2. शीशे का प्याला

I was searching for him all over the sky and
the earth
And he, in an innermost part of my heart had
his berth

The days of our union like moments fly
But the hours of separation like months lie

The heart discovers its nobleness in serving
the poor
This gem is just not found in a king's treasure

If you want love, look for a delicate heart.
It is a wine to be kept only in glass made pot

Keep quiet O heart, in the gathering shout not
Etiquette is the first lesson to be learnt in love's art.

I am one of my own critics, 'Iqbal',
So how can I call anyone small.

यूं तो ऐ बज़्म-ए-जहां दिलकश थे हंगामे तेरे
इक ज़रा अफ़सुर्दगी[1] तेरे तमाशाओं में थी

पा गई आसूदगी[2] कू-ए-मोहब्बत[3] में वो ख़ाक
मुद्दतों आवारा जो हिकमत[4] के सहराओं में थी

हुस्न की तासीर पर .गालिब न आ सकता था इल्म
इतनी नादानी जहां के सारे दानाओं में थी

मैंने 'इक़बाल' योरुप में उसे ढूंढा अबस
बात जो हिंदोस्तां के माह सीमाओं[5] में थी

Yun to ae bazmein-jahan dilkash the hungame tere
ik zara aphsurdgi tere tamashaon mein thi

Paa gayee aasoodgi ku-e-mohabbat mein woh khaaq
muddaton awara jo hikmat ke sehraon mein thi

Husn ki taseer per Ghalib na aa sakta the ilm
itnee nadaani jahan ke saare daanaon mein thi

Maine 'Iqbal' yorup mein use dhoondha abas
baat jo hindostan ke maahseemaon mein thi

---

1. उदासी 2. तुष्टि 3. प्रेम की गली 4. दर्शन 5. सुन्दर औरतों

Your fanfare, O world, is attractive though
There was a little sadness in the show even so

The dust that flitted about for long in the deserts
of philosophy
Found solace ultimately in love's alley

That knowledge couldn't have scored over the power
of beauty
All the wise men of the world had folly enough
to see

In vain, Iqbal, did I try in Europe to find
The charm that beauties in India bring to mind

न आते हमें इसमें तकरार क्या थी
मगर वादा करते हुए आर क्या थी

तुम्हारे पयामी ने सब राज़ खोला
ख़ता इसमें बंदे की सरकार क्या थी

ताम्मुल तो था उनको आने में क़ासिद
मगर यह बता तर्ज़-ए-इन्कार क्या थी

कहीं ज़िक्र रहता है 'इक़बाल' तेरा,
फ़सूँ[1] था कोई तेरी गुफ़तार क्या थी

Na aate humein ismein takraar kya thi
magar wada karte hue aar kya thi

Tumhare pyami ne sab raaz khola
khata ismein bande ki sarkar kya thi

Tammul to tha unko aane mein qasid
magar yeh bata tarz-e-inkaar kya thi

Kahin zikr rehta hai 'Iqbal' tera
phasoon tha koi teri guftaar kya thi

---

1. जादू

If you didn't want to come, I would not insist
But where was the problem in promising a visit

Your messenger gave it all away
What was my fault in it, tell me, pray

She was unwilling to come, alright, I know
But what was her mode of refusal, even so

They speak of you there, Iqbal so well
Your conversation has indeed cast a spell

रुबाई

तेरे सीने में दम है, दिल नहीं है
तेरा दम गर्मि-ए-महफिल नहीं है

गुज़र जा अक्ल के आगे कि ये नूर
चराग़े-राह है, मंज़िल नहीं है

तेरे शीशे में मय बाक़ी नहीं है
बता तू क्या मेरा साक़ी नहीं है

समुंदर से मिले प्यासे को शबनम
बख़ीली[1] है ये रज़्ज़ाक़ी[2] नहीं है

Tere seene mein dum hai, dil nahin hai
tera dum garmi-e-mehfil nahin hai

Guzar jaa aqal ke aage ki yeh noor
charage-raah hai, manzil nahin hai

Tere shishe mein mai baaki nahin hai
bata tu kya mera saaqi nahin hai

Samunder se mile pyase ko shabnam
bakhili hai ye razzaki nahin hai

---

1. मितव्ययी 2. उदार

A Rubai

There is breath in your chest, but no heart
And in warming up the mehfil, the breath has
no part

Transcend your reason because though it is a glow
It is not your destination, it can only the path to the
destination show

Is there no wine left in your chalice
Or is it that you are not my saqi

That the thirsty should get just a few dew drops from
the ocean,
It is niggardliness, certainly not generosity

तराना-ए-हिन्द

सारे जहाँ से अच्छा हिंदोस्ताँ हमारा
हम बुलबुलें हैं इसकी ये गुलिस्ताँ हमारा

गुरबत[1] में हों अगर हम, रहता है दिल वतन में
समझो वहीं हमें भी दिल हो जहाँ हमारा

परबत वो सबसे ऊंचा हमसाया आस्मां का
वो संतरी हमारा, वो पासबाँ[2] हमारा

गोदी में खेलती हैं इसकी हज़ारों नदियाँ
गुलशन है जिनके दम से रश्के-जिनाँ[3] हमारा

ऐ आबे-रौदे-गंगा! वो दिन हैं याद तुझको
उतरा तेरे किनारे जब कारवाँ हमारा

→

Saare jahan se achha hindostan humara
hum bulbulein hain iski ye gulistan humara

Ghurbat mein hon agar hum, rehta hai dil watan mein
samjho vahin humein bhi dil ho jahan humara

Parbat woh subse ooncha humsaya aasman ka
woh santari humara, woh paasbaan humara

Godi mein khelti hain iski hazaron nadiyan
gulshan hai jinke dum se rashq-e-jana humara

Ae aabe-raude-ganga ! woh din he yaad tujhko
utra tere kinare jab kaarwan humara

---

1. परदेस 2. रक्षक 3. स्वर्ग के लिए ईर्ष्या का कारण

Tarana-e-Hind : The Anthem of Hindustan

Better than the whole world is this Hindustan of ours
We are its nightingales, we sing in its bowers;

Even when we go abroad, at home we remain
in thought
For we are, where remains our heart?

Our sentinel it is, it is our protector
The mountain, higher than the high, the neighbour
of the sky;

In its lap a thousand streams play with glee
And make our garden bloom; make us the
heaven's envy

O you fast flowing waters of Ganga, do you remember
the day
When our caravan landed on your bank forever
to stay?

→

मज़हब नहीं सिखाता आपस में बैर रखना
हिंदी हैं हम वतन है हिंदोस्ताँ हमारा

यूनान-ओ-मिस्र-ओ-रोम [1] सब मिट गए जहाँ से
अब तक मगर है बाक़ी नामओ-निशाँ हमारा

कुछ बात है कि हस्ती मिटती नहीं हमारी
सदियों रहा है दुश्मन दौरे-ज़माँ [1] हमारा

'इक़बाल' कोई महरम [2] अपना नहीं जहाँ में
मालूम क्या किसी को दर्द-ए-निहाँ[3] हमारा

Mazhab nahin sikhata aapas mein bair rakhna
hindi hain hum, watan hai hindostan humara

Unaan-o-misr-o-roma sab mit gaye jahan se
ab tak magar hai baaqi namo-nishan humara

Kuchh baat hai ki hasti mitati nahin humari
sadiyon raha hai dushman daur-e-zaman humara

'Iqbal', koi marhum apna nahin jahan mein
maloom kya kisi ko dard-e-nihaan humara

---

1. संसार चक्र 2. भेदी 3. आंतरिक पीड़ा

Religion can never teach hatred, it must be
understood,
We all belong to India, and are bound by a common
motherhood

While the glories of Rome and Greece and Egypt are
a thing of the past
Our name and achievement still in the world last;

There is something in us that keeps us alive
For all the hostility of the world, we still survive

Nobody in the world, Iqbal, can share our sorrow
None can understand our grief, none can our
heartache know

नया शिवालय

सच कह दूं ऐ बिरहमन! गर तू बुरा न माने
तेरे सनमकदों के बुत हो गए पुराने

अपनों से बैर रखना तूने बुतों से सीखा
जंगा-ओ-जदल[1] सिखाया वाइज़ को भी ख़ुदा ने

तंग ओके मैंने आख़िर दैरा-ओ-हरम[2] को छोड़ा
वाइज़ का वाज़ छोड़ा, छोड़े तेरे फ़साने

पत्थर की मूरतों में समझा है तू ख़ुदा है
ख़ाके-वतन का मुझको हर ज़र्रा देवता है

आ ग़ैरियत के पर्दे एक बार फिर उठा दें
बिछड़ों को फिर मिला दें, नक़्श-ए-दुई मिटा दें

→

Such keh doon ae birhaman ! gar tu bura na maane
Tere sanamkadon ke but ho gaye purane

Apno se bair rakhna tune buton se seekha
Jang-o-jadal sikhaya vaiz ko bhi khuda ne

Tang aake maine aakhir dair-o-harum ko chhora
Vaiz ka vaaz chhora, chhore tere fasane

Pathar ki moorton mein samjha hai tu khuda hai
Khaake-watan ka mujhko her zarra devta hai

Aa ghairiyat ke parde ik baar phir utha dein
Bichhron ko phir mila dein, naqshe dui mita dein

---

1. युद्ध 2. मंदिर तथा काबे की चारदीवारी

The New Temple

If you don't mind O Brahmin, you should be told
That the idols in your temple have all grown old

You have learnt from them nothing but hostility
towards your own
To the maulvi also, God has only the path of
battle shown

I turned away from the temple because I was
fed up with it
And leaving the Kaba also, I thought, quite fit;

You think in these idols of stone resides the
God of thine
Every speck of my motherland's dust to me is divine

Let us once again this era of hostility end
Reunite the separated ones, towards unity our
energies bend

→

सूनी पड़ी हुई है मुद्दत से दिल की बस्ती
आ इक नया शिवाला इस देश में बना दें

दुनिया के तीर्थों से ऊंचा हो अपना तीरथ।
दामान-ए-आसमाँ से इसका कलश मिला दें

हर सुबह उठके गायें मंतर वो मीठे-मीठे
सारे पुजारियों को मय प्रीत की पिला दें

शक्ति भी, शांति भी, भक्तों के गीत में है
धरती के वासियों की मुक्ति प्रीत में है

Sooni pari hui hai muddat se dil ki basti
Aa ik naya shivalaya is desh mein bana dein

Duniya ke tirthon mein ooncha ho apna tirath
Daamane-aasman se iska kalash mila dein

Her subah uthke gaayen manter woh meethe-meethe
Saare pujariyon ko mai preet ki pila dein

Shakti bhi, shanti bhi, bhakton ke geet mein hai
Dharti ke vasiyon ki mukti preet mein hai

For ages now, our heart is in a dreary state
Let us now a temple new in this country create

With its dome touching the sky
Let our pilgrim place be higher than the high;

Let us sing every morning mantras sweet,
Let every priest now on have love's surfeit

Our song of devotion now should give us strength
and peace
And in love alone should lie our final release

हुआ ख़ेमाज़न कारवान-ए-बहार
इरम बन गया दामन-ए-कोहसार

फ़िज़ा नीली-नीली, हवा में सुरूर
ठहरते नहीं आशियां में तुयूर

वो जूए-कोहिस्तां उचकती हुई
मचलती लचकती सरकती हुई

उछलती फिसलती संभलती हुई
बड़े पेंच खाकर निकलती हुई

रुके जब तो सिल चीर देती है ये
पहाड़ों के दिल चीर देती है ये

ज़रा देख ऐ साक़िय-ए-लालाफ़ाम
सुनाती है ये ज़िदंगी का पयाम

पिलादे मुझे वो मय-ए-पर्दा-सोज़
कि आती नहीं फ़स्ले-गुल रोज़-रोज़

→

Hua khemazan kaarwane-bahaar
Iram ban gaya daamne-kohsaar

Fiza neeli-neeli, hawa mein saroor
Theharte nahin aashiyan mein tuyoor

Woh jue-kohastan uchakti hui
Machalti lachakti sarakti hui

Uchhalti fisalti sambhalti hui
Bare pech khakar nikatli hui

Ruke jab to sil cheer deti hai ye
Paharon ke dil cheer deti hai ye

Jara dekh ae saakiye-laalafaam
Sunati hai ye zindagi ka payaam

Pilade mujhe woh maye-parda-soz
Ki aati nahin fasle-gul roz-roz

To The Saqi

The spring has arrived and pitched its tent,
And hillside a veritable paradise,

The skies are blue and intoxicating the breeze
The birds feel like flying up from their nests

Down from the hill comes the rill sliding
Leaping, hopping, stumbling, moving

Slipping, creeping, recovering, flowing,

It pierces the rock, if it's blocked
It tears apart the mountain's heart

O rose-like Saqi, may you hear
The life's message is coming clear

O pour me the fiery wine which tears the veil apart
For everyday the rose-season visits not.

→

वो मय जिससे रोशन ज़मीरे-हयात
वो मय जिससे है मस्ती-ए-कायनात

वो मय जिसमें है सोज़-ओ-साज़-ए अज़ल
वो मय जिससे खुलता है राज़-ए-अज़ल

उठा साक़िया पर्दा इस राज़ से
लड़ादे ममोले को शहबाज़ से

ज़माने के अंदाज़ बदले गये
नया राग है साज़ बदले गये

पुरानी सियासत गिरी .ख्वार है
ज़मीं मीर-ओ-सुलताँ से बेज़ार है

गया दौर-ए-सरमायादारी गया
तमाशा दिखाकर मदारी गया

गरां:ख्वाब चीनी संभलने लगे
हिमालय के चश्मे उबलने लगे

→

Woh mai jisse roshan zamire-hayaat
Woh mai jisse hai masti-e-kaaynaat

Woh mai jismein hai soz-o-saaz-e azal
Woh mai jisse khulta hai raaz-e-azal

Utha saqiya parda is raaz se
Lara de mamole ko shehbaaz se

Zamane ke andaaz badle gaye
Naya raag hai saaz badle gaye

Purani siyasat giri khawar hai
Zamin meer-o-sultaan se bezaar hai

Gaya daur-e-sarmay-dari gaya
Tamasha dikhakar madari gaya

Garaan-khawab Cheeni sambhalne lage
Himalaya ke chashme ubalne lage

The wine that brightens the soul with light
The wine that is the world's delight

The wine of warmth and raptures great
The wine that reveals life innate

Remove the veil O Saqi, from that sight
And let the little sparrow challenge the falcon's might

The ways of the world are beginning to change
New melodies flow from instruments new

The politics of yore has run its course
Sick and tired of them, the world wants kings
and nobles to go

Out of steam has capitalism run
Out goes the juggler, his tricks all gone

Himalayan springs are boiling hot
And the Chinese awake from deep slumber at last

→

शराब-ए-कुहन फिर पिला साक़िया
वही जाम गर्दिश में ला साक़िया

मुझे इश्क़ के पर लगा कर उड़ा
मेरी ख़ाक जुगनू बना कर उड़ा

खिरद को ग़ुलामी से आज़ाद कर
जवानों को पीरों का उस्ताद कर

जिगर से वही तीर फिर पार कर
तमन्ना को सीनों में बेदार कर

तेरे आसमानों के तारों की ख़ैर
ज़मीनों के शब ज़िंदादारों की ख़ैर

जवानों को सोज़-ए-जिगर बख़्श दे
मेरा इश्क़, मेरी नज़र बख़्श दे

मेरी नाव गिरदाब से पार कर
ये सावत है तू इसको सय्यार कर

→

Sharabe-kuhan phir pila saqiya
Wahi jaam gardish mein laa saqiya

Mujhe ishq ke per laga kar ura
Meri khaaq jugnoo bana kar ura

Khird ko ghulami se azaad kar
Jawanon ko peeron ka ustaad kar

Jigar se wahi teer phir paar kar
Tamanna ko seenon mein bedaar kar

Tere aasmanon ke taaron ki khair
Zaminon ke shab zindadaron ki khair

Jawanon ko soze-jigar bakhsh de
Mera ishq, meri nazar bakhsh de

Miri naao girdaab se paar kar
Yeh sabut hai tu isko sayyar kar

Pour me O Saqi that wine of old
Let that cup go round once more,

On the wings of love, let me fly
Let my dust a firefly be

Set us free from intellectual slavery
And let the youth be our teacher

Pierce us again with arrow smart
Let a powerful longing awake in our heart

May the stars in sky be blessed
May their light be never blocked

Fill with fire the youthful hearts
Let them feel my passion, my love,

Out of the whirlpool, pull my boat
Still it is intact, set it afloat

→

बता मुझको असरार-ए-मर्गे-ए-हयात
कि तेरी निगाहों में है कायनात

मेरे दीदाए-तर की बेख़्वाबियां
मेरे दिल की पोशीदा बेताबियां

उमंगें मेरी, आरज़ूएँ मेरी
उमीदें मेरी जुस्तजूएँ मेरी

मेरी फ़ितरत आईना-ए-रोज़गार
ग़ज़ालाने अफ़कार का मर्ग़ज़ार

मेरा दिल, मेरी रज़्मगाहे हयात
गुमानों को लश्कर यक़ीं का सबात—

यही कुछ है साक़ी मताए फ़क़ीर
इसी से फ़क़ीरी में हूँ मैं अमीर

मेरे क़ाफ़िले में लुटा दे इसे
लुटा दे ठिकाने लगा दे इसे

Bata mujhko asraare-marg-e-hayaat
Ki teri nigahon mein hai kaaynaat

Mere deeda-e-tar ki bekhabiyan
Mere dil ki poshida betabiyan

Umange meri, aarzuen meri
Umeeden meri, just juen meri

Meri fitrat aaina-e-rozgar
Gazalaane aphkaar ka margzaar

Mera dil, meri razmgahe hayaat
Gumanon ko lashkar yaqin ko sabaat

Yahi kuchh hai saaqi mataae faqir
Isee se faqiri mein hoon main ameer

Mere qafile mein luta de ise
Luta de, thikane laga de ise

Mystery of life, mystery of death
You do know, so let me know

My tearful eye hardly sleeps
My heart's anguish is unseen though

My midnights' cry, my burning heart
Lonely in crowd, my tearful eye

My desires, my hope, my quest restless
My nature that mirrors that world at work

My heart, my battlefield of life
Battalions of doubt, my faith steadfast

This sums up the mendicant's wealth
Because of which I am rich indeed

On my caravan shower it all
Let it on its right place fall.

तस्वीरे-दर्द

नहीं मिन्नत-कश-ए-ताबे-शुनीदन[1] दास्तां मेरी
ख़मोशी गुफ़्तगू है, बेज़ुबानी है ज़ुबां मेरी

ये दस्तूर-ए-ज़ुबाँबंदी है कैसा तेरी महफ़िल में
यहां तो बात करने को तरसती है ज़ुबां मेरी

उठाए कुछ वरक़ लाला ने, कुछ नर्गिस ने, कुछ गुल ने
चमन में हर तरफ़ बिखरी हुई है दास्ताँ मेरी

उड़ा ली क़ुमरियों ने, तूतियों ने, अंदलीबों ने
चमन वालों ने मिलकर लूट ली तर्ज़-ए-फ़ुग़ाँ[2] मेरी

→

Nahin minnat-kash-e-taabe-shunidan daastan meri
Khamcshi guftgu hai, bezabani hai zabaan meri

Ye dastur-e-zabanbandi hai kaisa teri mehfil mein
Yahan to baat karne ko tarasti hai zabaan meri

Uthae kuchh warq laala ne, kuchh nargis ne, kuchh gul ne
Chaman mein her taraf bikhri hui hai daastan meri

Ura lee qumriyon ne, tutiyon ne, andlibon ne
Chaman walon ne milkar loot lee tarz-e-phugaan meri

---

1. सुनने की शक्ति की आभारी 2. आर्तनाद का ढंग

A Picture of Anguish

I am not begging anybody to hear my tale
My silence is eloquent, my voicelessness, my tongue

O what a gag on speech in the assembly of yours
That I should yearn to speak and cannot utter a
word here

Each one of these various flowers has plucked a leaf
from my book
And the garden is strewn with my tale everywhere

The peacock, the parrot and the cuckoo, these
residents of the garden
All have robbed me of my sighs; have robbed me
of my song
→

टपक ऐ शम्मअ! आंसू बन के परवानों की आंखों से
सरापा[1] दर्द हूं, हसरत-भरी है दास्ताँ मेरी

इलाही फिर मज़ा क्या है यहां दुनिया में रहने का
हयात-ए-जाविदां[2] मेरी न मर्गे-नागहाँ[3] मेरी

मेरा रोना नहीं, रोना है ये सारे गुलिस्तां का
वो गुल हूं मैं ख़िज़ां हर गुल की है गोया ख़िज़ाँ मेरी

Tapak ae shamma ! aansu ban ke parwanon ki aankhon se
Sarapa dard hoon, hasrat-bhari hai daastan meri

Ilahi phir maza kya hai yahan duniya mein rehne ka
Hayat-e-jaadan meri na marg-e-naaghaan meri

Mera rona nahin rona hai ye saare gulistan ka
Woh gul hoon main khizan her gul ki hai goya
khizan meri

1. सिर से पैर तक 2. अमर जीवन 3. आकस्मिक मृत्यु

Flow, O candle from the eyes of the moth, O weep
For, I am anguish incarnate, my tale is full of grief

What is the fun of living in this world, O Lord!
When I command neither life eternal nor my death

My lamentation is not mine alone; it is the lamentation
of the whole garden
For, every flower's autumn is my own autumn

निशान-ए-बर्ग-ए-गुल[1] *तक भी न छोड़ा बाग़ में गुलचीं*[2]
तेरी क़िस्मत से रज़्म-आराइयां[3] *हैं बाग़बानों में*

छुपाकर आस्तीं में बिजलियां रख दी हैं गर्दूं[4] *ने*
अनादिल[5] *बाग़ के ग़ाफ़िल न बैठें आशियानों में*

सुन ऐ ग़ाफ़िल! सदा मेरी, यह ऐसी चीख़ है जिसको
वज़ीफ़ा[6] *जानकर पढ़ते हैं तायर*[7] *बोस्तानों*[8] *में*

वतन की फ़िक्र कर नादां! मुसीबत आने वाली है
तेरी बर्बादियों के मश्वरे हैं आस्मानों में

ज़रा देख उसको जो कुछ हो रहा है होने वाला है
धरा क्या है भला अहद-ए-कुहन[9] *की दास्तानों में*

न समझोगे तो मिट जाओगे ऐ हिंदोस्तां वालो!
तुम्हारी दास्तां तक भी न होगी दास्तानों में

Nishan-e-barg-e-gul tak bhi na chhora baag mein gulchin
Teri qismat se razm-aaraaiyan hain baghbaanon mein

Chhupakar aastinon mein bijliyan rakhdi hain gardu ne
Anadil baagh ke ghafil ne baithen aashiyanon mein

Sun ae ghafil ! sada meri, yeh aisee cheekh hai jisko
Wazifa jaankar padhte hain taayer bostaano mein

Vatan ki fikr kar nadaan ! musibat aane wali hai
Teri barbadiyon ke mashware hain aasmaanon mein

Zara Dekh usko jo kuchh ho raha hai, hone wala hai
Dhara kya hai bhala ahade-kuhan ki daastanon mein

Ne samjhoge to mit jaaoge ae hindostan walon !
Tumhari daastan tak bhi na hogi daastanon mein

---

1. फूल की पंखुरी का चिह्न 2. माली 3. झगड़े 4. आकाश 5. बुलबुल 6. जाप 7. पक्षी 8. बागों 9. पुराने जमाने

You have not left any trace of flowers behind,
O gardener,
You have, instead, sown discord everywhere

Heavens are hiding lightning in their sleeves
The nightingales must not remain oblivious in their
nests in the garden

Hear, O thou indifferent one, for, such is
my exhortation
That the birds repeat it in their prayers in the garden

Think of the nation, thou ignorant one, the trouble
in brewing
And plans of your destruction are being hatched in
heaven

Keep your eye on what is happening now and events
that in future lie
No use dwelling on glory of ages gone by

If you don't wake up now, you people of Hindustan
From the annals of the world you will be for
ever gone

हुवेदा[1] आज अपने ज़ख़्मे-पिनहां[2] करके छोड़ूंगा
लहू रो रो के महफ़िल को गुलिस्तां करके छोड़ूंगा

जलाना है मुझे हर शम्मअ-दिल को सोज़-ए-पिनहां[3] से
तेरी तारीक रातों में चिराग़ां करके छोड़ूंगा

पिरोना एक ही तसबीह[4] में इन बिखरे दानों को।
जो मुश्किल है तो इस मुश्किल को आसां करके छोड़ूंगा॥

जो है पर्दों में पिनहां, चश्मे-बीना[5] देख लेती है
ज़माने की तबीयत का तक़ाज़ा देख लेती है

Huveda aaj apne zakhm-e-pinhan karke chhorunga
Lahoo ro ro ke mehfil ko gulistan karke chhorunga

Jalana hai mujhe her shamma-e-dil ko soz-e-pinhan se
Teri tareek raaton mein chiragan karke chhorunga

Pirona ek hi tasbeeh mein in bikhre daano ko
Jo mushkil hai to is mushkil ko aasaan karke chhorunga

Jo hai pardon mein pinhan, chashme-beena dekh ltehai
Zamane ki tabiyat ka taqaza dekh leti hai

1. प्रकट 2. छुपे हुए घाव 3. भीतर की आग 4. माला 5. देखने वाली आंख

I will make my wounds bare today
I will shed tears of blood and colour the mehfil red

I'll light an inner fire in every heart
And illuminate the nights pitch-dark

I will string together these scattered beads
And if it is difficult indeed, I'll make it look easy

He who sees beneath the surface, insightful
man is he
He sees what the world wants to see but cannot see

किया रफ़अत[1] की लज़्ज़त से न दिल को आशना तूने
गुज़ारी उम्र पस्ती में मिसाल-ए-नक़्शे-पा[2] तूने

फ़िदा करता रहा दिल को हसीनों की अदाओं पर
मगर देखी न इस आईने में अपनी अदा तूने

दिखा वो हुस्न-ए-आलम-सोज़[3] अपनी चश्म-ए-पुरनम[4] को
जो तड़पाता है परवाने को, रुलवाता है शबनम को

तेरा नज़्ज़ारा ही ऐ बुल्हवस![5] मक़सद नहीं इसका
बनाया है किसी ने कुछ समझकर चश्म-ए-आदम[6] को

→

Kiya rafát ki lazzat se na dil ko aashana tune
Guzari umr pasti mein misal-e-naksh-e-paa tune

Fida karta raha dil ko hasinon ki adaaon par
Magar dekhi na is aaine mein apni ada tune

Dikha woh husn-e-aalam-soz apni chashm-e-purnam ko
Jo tarapata hai parwane ko, rulwata he shabnam ko

Tera Nazara hi ae bulhavas ! maqsad nahin iska
Banaya hai kisi ne kuchh samajhkar chashme-aadam ko

---

1. बुलंदी 2. पैरों के निशान की तरह 3. दुनिया को जलाने वाली सुंदरता 4. भीगी आंखों 5. लोलुप 6. मनुष्य की आंख

You have not known the joy of flying high
And like a foot-print, lead a lowly life

You have been losing your heart to the beauties
around
And never the beauty in your own heart you found.

Show your tearful eye the beauty that lights
the world
The beauty that makes the moth restless, make the
dew shed tears

Your aim is not to see the surroundings only, you
lowly one
The human eye is made for loftier destination;

→

शजर[1] है फ़िर्क़ा-आराई[2] तअस्सुब[3] है समर[4] इसका
ये वो फल है कि जन्नत से निकलवाता है आदम को

फिरा करते नहीं मजरूह-ए-उल्फ़त[5] फ़िक्र-ए-दरमां[6] में
ये जख़्मी आप कर लेते हैं पैदा अपने मरहम को

बियाबान-ए-मोहब्बत[7] दश्ते-गुरबत[8] भी, वतन भी है
यह वीराना क़फ़स भी, आशियाना भी, चमन भी है

मोहब्बत ही वो मंज़िल है कि मंज़िल भी है सहरा भी
जरस[9] भी, कारवां भी, राहबर[10] भी, राहज़न भी है

Shajar hai phirqa-aaraai tássub hai samar iska
Ye woh phal hai ki jannat se nikalwata hai aadam ko

Phira karte nahin majrooh-e-ulfat phikr-e-darman mein
Ye zakhmi aap kar late hain paida apne marhum ko

Biyaban-e-mohabbat dashte-gurbat bhi, vatan bhi hai
Yeh virana qafas bhi, aashiyana bhi, chaman bhi hai

Mohabbat hi woh manzil hai ki manzil bhi hai
sehra bhi
Jaras bhi, kaarvan bhi, raahbar bhi, raahzan bhi hai

---

1. वृक्ष 2. सांप्रदायिकता 3. विद्वेष 4. फल 5. प्रेम के घायल 6. चिकित्सा की तलाश 7. प्रेम का मरुस्थल 8. परदेस का जंगल 9. घड़ियाल 10. पथ-प्रदर्शक

If the tree is a tree of communalism, enmity is going
to be its fruit
And this is the fruit that causes man's expulsion
from heaven

Those wounded in love, are not bothered about
looking for the cure around
They themselves produce the balm for their wound

Love is at once a cage, a nest and a garden blooming,
Its odyssey takes us to the land of exile, as also
to our homeland

A gong, a caravan, a guide, a robber, all at once
Love is a journey, which can end in the desert sand.

फ़र्मान-ए-खुदा फ़रिश्तों के नाम

उट्ठो मेरी दुनिया के ग़रीबों को जगा दो
काख़-ए-उमरा[1] के दरो-दीवार हिला दो

गरमाओ गुलामों का लहू सोज़-ए-यक़ीं से
कुंजश्क-ए-फ़रोमाया[2] को शाहीं से लड़ा दो

सुलतानी-ए-जमहूर[3] का आता है ज़माना
जो नक़्शे-कुहन[4] तुमको नज़र आये मिटा दो

जिस खेत से दहक़ां[5] को मयस्सर नहीं रोज़ी
उस खेत के हर ख़ोशा-ए-गंदुम को जला दो

मैं नाखुश-ओ-बेज़ार हूं मरमर की सिलों से
मेरे लिए मिट्टी का हरम और बना दो

Uththo meri duniya ke garibon ko jaga do
Kaakh-e-umra ke dar-o-deewar hila do

Garmao ghulamon ka lahoo soz-e-yaqin se
Kunjashk-e-faromaya ko shahin se lara do

Sultani-e-jamhoor ka aata hai zamana
Jo naqshe-kuhan tumko nazar aaye mita do

Jis khet se dehqaan ko maissar nahin rozi
Us khet ke her ghosha-e-gandum ko jala do

Main nakhush-o-bezaar hun marmar ki silon se
Mere liye mitti ka harum aur bana do

1. अमीरों के महल 2. एक छोटी चिड़िया 3. गणराज्य 4. पुरातन चिह्न 5. निर्धन

God's Command (To the Angles)

Rise thou now and wake up the poor of my world
Shake from their foundations the palaces of rich

Warm thou now the blood of the slaves with the
fire of faith
And make the meek sparrow take the falcon on;

The age of the common man is approaching fast
Blot out all the emblems of the past that you sight

Burn every corn of wheat growing in the field
That provides not for the tiller's need

I am sick of seeing its columns laid in marble
Build for me a Kaba now of clay and mud

ज़माना

जो था नहीं है, जो है न होगा, यही है एक हर्फ़े-महरमाना[1]
क़रीबतर है नमूद[2] *जिसकी उसी का मुश्ताक़ है ज़माना*

मेरी सुराही से क़तरा-क़तरा नए हवादिस[3] *टपक रहे हैं*
मैं अपनी तसबीहे-रोज़ो-शब[4] *का शुमार करता हूं दाना दाना*

हर एक से आशना हूं लेकिन जुदा-जुदा रस्मो-राह मेरी
किसी का राकिब[5] *किसी का मुरकिब*[6]*, किसी को इबरत का ताज़ियाना*[7]

न था अगर तू शरीके-महफ़िल क़ुसूर मेरा है या कि तेरा?
मेरा तरीक़ा नहीं कि रख लूं किसी की ख़ातिर मये-शबाना[8]

→

Jo tha nahin hai, jo hai na hoga, yahi hai ek harphe meharmana
Kareebtar hai namood jiski usee ka mushtaq hai zamana

Meri surahi se qatra-qatra naye hawadis tapak rahe hain
Main apni tasbeehe-rozo-shab ka shumaar karta hun daana-daana

Her ek se aashna hun lekin juda-juda rasmo-raah meri
Kisi ka raaqib kisi ka murkib, kisi ko ibrat ka taaziyana

Na tha agar tu sharike-mehfil qusoor mera hai ya ki tera

Mera tariqa nahin ki rakh loon kisi ke khatir maye-shabana

---

1. अपराध से भरा शब्द 2. उत्पत्ति 3. दुर्घटनाएं 4. दिन-रात की माला 5. सवार 6. सवारी 7. कोड़ा 8. रात की शराब

The Changing Times

What was, is not, what is, will not be—that is the
unpleasant truth—
The world looks forward to that which is
unfolding now,

Drop by drop, from my pitcher, tragedies drip
As the beads of rosary of day and night slip,

I am friendly with everybody, from everybody
differently cast—
Rider to the one, carrier to the other, to the third
a whiplash severe,

If you were not a part of the mehfil, was it your fault
or mine?
It is not my wont to keep for somebody the night's
wine;

→

हवाएं उनकी, फ़ज़ाएं उनकी, समन्दर उनके, जहाज़ उनके
गिरह भंवर की खुले तो क्योंकर, भंवर है तकदीर का बहाना

जहाने-नौ[1] हो रहा है पैदा वो आलमे-पीर[2] मर रहा है
जिसे फ़िरंगी मुक़ामिरों[3] ने बना दिया है क़मारख़ाना[4]

हवा है गो तेज़-ओ-तुंद लेकिन चिराग़ अपना जला रहा है
वो मर्दे-दरवेश[5] जिसको हक़[6] ने दिये हैं अंदाज़े-ख़ुसरवाना[7]

Hawaen unki, fazaen unki, samandar unke, jahaaz unke
Girah bhanwar ki khule to kyonkar, bhanwar hai taqdeer ka bahana

Jahane-nau ho raha hai paida woh aalme-peer mar raha hai
Jise firangi muqamiron ne bana diya hai qamaarkhana

Hawa hi go tez-o-tund lekin chirag apna jala raha hai
Woh marde-darvesh jisko huq ne diye hain andaze khusrawana

1. नया संसार 2. बूढ़ा ज़माना 3. जूएबाज़ 4. जूआखाना 5. साधु 6. भगवान 7. बादशाहों के अंदाज़

Theirs are the breezes; theirs the sky, the ships and
the ocean belong to them
How can we control the whirlpool, which is another
name for fate, then?

A new world is taking birth old one is dying
It's a world that the gamblers of Europe are using
as their den;

The sage whom God has given a royal temper,
even so
Lights his candle, though the stormy breezes blow.

फ़ल्सफ़ा-ए-ग़म

एक भी पत्ती अगर कम हो तो वो गुल ही नहीं
जो ख़िज़ां-नादीदा[1] हो बुलबुल वो बुलबुल ही नहीं
आरज़ू के ख़ून से रंगीं है दिल की दास्तां
नग़मा-ए-इन्सानियत कामिल[2] नहीं ग़ैर-अज़-फ़ुग़ां[3]
ग़म जवानी को जगा देता है लुत्फ़े-ख़्वाब से
साज़ यह बेदार होता है इसी मिज़राब से

शाम जिसकी आशना-ए-नाला-ए-'या-रब'[4] नहीं
जल्वा-पैरा[5] जिसकी शब में अश्क के कोकब[6] नहीं
हाथ जिस गुलचीं का है महफ़ूज़ नोके-ख़ार से
इश्क़ जिसका बेख़बर है हिज्र के आज़ाब[7] से
कुल्फ़ते-ग़म[8] गर्चे उसके रोज़ो-शब से दूर है
ज़िन्दगी का राज़ उसकी आंख से मस्तूर[9] है

→

Ek bhi patti agar kam ho to woh gul hi nahin
jo khizaan-nadeeda ho bulbul woh bulbul hi nahin
Aarzu ke khoon se rangin hai dil ki daastan
naghma-e-insaniyat kamil nahin gair-az-fugan
Gham jawani ko jaga deta hai lutfe-khawab se
saaz yeh bedaar hota hai isee mizraab se

Sham jiski aashana-e-nala-e-'ya-rub' nahin
jalwa-paira jiski shab mein ask ke kokab nahin
Haath jis gulchin ka hai mehfooz noke-khar se
ishq jiska bekhabar hai hijr ke aazaab se
Kulfate gham garche uske rozo-shab se door hai
zindagi ka raaz uski aankh se mastoor hai

---

1. पतझड़ न देखी हो 2. पूरा 3. बिना आर्तनाद के 4. जो व्यक्ति शाम के समय 'हे भगवान' कहकर दुखी न हुआ हो 5. प्रदर्शित 6. सितारे 7. कष्ट 8. ग़म का संताप 9. छुपा हुआ

Philosophy of Sorrow

The rose, even if it is one petal short, is no
rose at all
As the nightingale that has not the autumn seen
Cannot be a nightingale called;
The death of dreams characterizes the story of
the heart.
The song of humanity is incomplete without
sighs and sobs,
Sorrow wakes up a man from slothful sleep
Only from this instrument comes out a melody deep.

One who has not cried in the evening and
prayed to God
One whose evenings are not lit up with tears like
the stars
A gardener whose finger has not bled by a sharp
thorn
A man who has not the pangs of separation
undergone
His days and nights might not have been scalded
by sorrow though,
Such a person can never the secrets of life know.

→

रुख़सत-ए-महबूब का मक़सद फ़ना होता अगर
जोश-ए-उल्फ़त भी दिल-ए-आशिक़ से कर जाता सफ़र
इश्क़ कुछ महबूब के मरने से मर जाता नहीं
रूह में ग़म बनके रहता है मगर जाता नहीं

आती है नद्दी जबीन-ए-कोह[1] से गाती हुई
आस्मां के तायरों[2] को नग़्मा सिखलाती हुई
आइना रोशन है उसकी सूरते-रुख़्सार-हूर
गिरके वादी की चटानों पर से हो जाता है चूर
नहर जो थी उसके गौहर प्यारे-प्यारे बन गए
यानी इस उफ्ताद[3] से पानी के तारे बन गए॥
जू-ए-सीमाब-ए-रवां[4] फटकर परेशां हो गई
मुज़्तरिब[5] बूंदों की इक दुनियां नुमायां हो गई
पस्ती-ए-आलम में मिलने को जुदा होते हैं हम
आर्ज़ी फ़ुर्क़त को दायम[6] जानकर रोते हैं हम

→

Rukhsat-e-mehboob ka maqsad fana hota agar
josh-e-ulfat bhi dil-e-aashiq se kar jaata safar
Ishq kuchh mehboob ke marne se mar jaata nahin
rooh mein gham banke rehta hai magar jaata nahin

Aati hai naddi jabin-e-koh se gaati hui
aasmaan ke taayron ko naghma sikhlati hui
Aaina roshan hai uski surat-e-rukhsar-e-hoor
girke vadi ki chattano per ye ho jaata hai choor
Nehar jo thi uske gauhar pyare-pyare ban gaye
yaani is uftaad se paani ke taare ban gaye
Ju-e-seemab-e-rawan phatkar pareshan ho gayee
muztarib boondon ki ik duniyan numayan ho gayee
Aarazi bhurkat ko dayam jaankar roten hai hum

---

1. पर्वत-शिखर से 2. पक्षियों 3. दुर्घटना 4. बहते हुए पारे की नदी 5. व्याकुल 6. स्थायी

If the departure of the loved one were the end of the game
Love's passion too would have departed from the lover's heart
Love is not something that dies with the beloved's demise
It survives in the form of grief, it dies not.

From the mountain peak, the stream that comes
Stirring the birds in the sky into melody
Shining like the cheek of a fairy,
Breaks into pieces and falls on the rock in the valley—
The sheet of flowing water has been rent apart,
But the seeming tragedy has become a sky of twinkling stars
And a new world of bubbling waters has come into view,
At the end of every inning in this world, we separate to meet again
By taking the temporary parting as permanent, we cry in vain

→

मरने वाले मरते हैं लेकिन फ़ना होते नहीं
ये हक़ीक़त में कभी हमसे जुदा होते नहीं

अक़्ल जिस दम दहर[1] की आफ़ात[2] में महसूर[3] हो
या जवानी की अंधेरी रात में मस्तूर[4] हो

ख़िज़्र-ए-हिम्मत[5] हो गया हो आरज़ू से गोशागीर
फ़िक्र जब आजिज़ हो और ख़ामोश आवाज़-ए-ज़मीर[6]

वादी-ए-हस्ती में कोई हमसफ़र तक भी न हो
जादह[7] दिखलाने को जुगनू का शरर तक भी न हो

मरने वाले की जबीं रोशन है इस ज़ुल्मात में
जिस तरह तारे चमकते हैं अंधेरी रात में

Marne wale marte hain lekin fana hote nahin
ye haqiqat mein kabhi humse juda hote nahin

Aql jis dam dehar ki aafaat mein mehsoor ho
ya jawani ki andheri raat mein mastoor ho

Khizr-e-himmat ho gaya ho aarzu se goshageer
fikr jab aajiz ho aur khamosh aawaz-e-zameer

Vadi-e-hasti mein koi humsafar tak bhi ni ho
Jaadah dikhlane ko jugnoo ka sharar tak bhi na ho

Marne wale ki jabin roshan hai is zulmaat main
jis tarah taare chamakte hain andheri raat mein

---

1. दुनिया 2. मुसीबत 3. घिरी हुई 4. छुपी हुई 5. साहस का नेता 6. आत्मा की आवाज़
7. राह

Those who die perish not
Their physical separation from us is no
separation at all

Whenever we are overwhelmed by the sorrows of
the world

When the death of a young one darkens our vision
And we are losing heart
When grief our consciousness numbs

When we feel starkly lonely
And not even a firefly shows us the way—

The face of dead man even in this gloom wears
a glow
As stars in darkness to the traveller, his way show.

रात और शायर

क्यों मेरी चाँदनी में फिरता है तू परेशाँ
ख़ामोश सूरत-ए-गुल, मानन्द-ए-बू परेशां
तारों के मोतियों का शायद है जौहरी तू
मछली है कोई मेरे दरिया-ए-नूर की तू
या तू मिरी जबीं का तारा गिरा हुआ है
रिफ़अत को छोड़कर जो पस्ती में जा बसा है

ख़ामोश हो गया है तारे-रुबाबे-हस्ती
है मेरे आईने में तस्वीरे-ख़्वाबे हस्ती
दरिया की तह में चश्म-ए-गिरदाब सो गई है
साहिल से लग के मौज-ए-बेताब सो गई है
बस्ती ज़मीं की कैसी हंगामा-आफ़री[1] है
यों सो गई है जैसे आबाद ही नहीं है
शायर का दिल है लेकिन ना-आशना सकूं से
आज़ाद रह गया तू क्योंकर मिरे फ़सूं से

Kyon meri chandni mein phirta hai tu pareshan
khamosh surat-e-gul, manande bu pareshan
Taron ke motiyon ka shayad hai johri tu
machhli hai koi mere dariya-e-noor ki tu
Ya tu miri jabin ka tara gira hua hai
rifát ko chhorkar jo pasti mein ja basa hai

Khamosh ho gaya hai taare-rubabe hasti
hai mere aayne mein tasvir-e-khawabe hasti
Dariya ki teh mein chashme-girdaab so gayee hai
sahil se lag ke mauje-betaab so gayee hai
Basti zamin ki kaisi hungama-aafarin hai
yon so gayee hai jaise aabaad hi nahin hai
Shayar ka dil he lekin na-aashana sakoon
azaad reh gaya tu kyonkar mire fasun se

---
1. हलचल मचाने वाली

The Night to the Poet

Why are you roaming in my moonlight distraught
Quiet like a flower, like its fragrance scattered?
You are a jeweller perhaps dealing in pearl-like stars
Or you are a fish swimming in the river of my light
Or a star fallen from my brow
Fallen from the height into the territory low!

The music of life has fallen asleep
Asleep in fact is life itself,
And at the bottom of the river sleeps the vortex.
Full of sound and storm otherwise,
The very life sleeps as if no one here resides;
How come, you escape my magic touch,
How come the poet's heart has no rest!

मैं तेरे चांद की खेती में गुहर बोता हूं
छिप के इंसानों से मानन्दे-सहर रोता हूं
दिन की शोरिश में निकलते हुए शर्माते हैं
उज़लत-ए-शब [1] में मेरे अश्क टपक जाते हैं

मुझ में फ़रयाद जो पिनहां हैं सुनाऊं किसको
तपिश-ए-शौक़ का नज़्ज़ारा दिखाऊं किसको?
बर्क़-ए-ऐमन मिरे सीने में पड़ी रोती है
देखने वाली जो है आँख कहीं सोती है?

सिफ़ते-शमअे-लहद मुर्दा है महफ़िल मेरी
आह ऐ रात! बड़ी दूर है मंज़िल मेरी–
अहदे-हाज़िर की हवा रास नहीं है इसको
अपने नुकसान का एहसास नहीं है इसको
ज़ब्त-ए-पैग़ाम-ए-मुहब्बत से जो घबराता हूं
तेरे ताबिंदा सितारों को सुना जाता हूं

Main tere chand ki kheti mein guhar bota hun
chhip ke insano se maanande-sehar rota hoon
Din ki shorish mein nikalte hue sharmate hain
uzalt-e-shab mein mere ashk tapak jaate hain

Mujh mein faryad jo pinhaan hai sunaun kisko
tapish-e-shauq ka nazara dikhaun kisko?
Barq-aeman mere seene mein pari roti hai
dekhne wali jo hai aankh kahin soti hai

Sifte-shamá-lahad murda hai mehfil meri
aah ae raat ! bari door hai manzil meri
Ahd-e-hazir ki hawa raas nahin hai isko
apne nuqsaan ka ahsaas nahin hai isko
Zabt-e-paighaamein-e-muhabbat se jo ghabrata hun
tere tabinda sitaron ko suna jaata hoon

---

1. रात के एकांत में 2. बजली

The Poet

I sow pearls in the expanse of your moonlight
Hidden from the people's eye, like the dawn, I weep,
My tears, hesitant to show in the light of the day
Tend to flow in the solitude of night,

O where should I lighten my heart's burden?
The lightning of mount Sinai in my chest sobs
How can the Seeing Eye slumber in peace at night?

Desolate like the candle of the grave, my *mehfil* lies
And far, far away is my destination, O night.
The climate of present times suits me not
Of its heavy loss, the world has no thought,
When my message of love, no longer can I hold
in my heart
I come and deliver it to your shining stars.

साक़ी

नशा पिलाके गिराना तो सबको आता है
मज़ा तो जब है कि गिरतों को थाम ले साक़ी

जो बादाकश थे पुराने वो उठते जाते हैं
कहीं से आब-ए-बक़ा-ए-दवाम[1] ले साक़ी

कटी है रात तो हंगामा-गुस्तरी में[2] तेरी
सहर क़रीब है अल्लाह का नाम ले साक़ी

Nasha pilake girana to subko aata hai
Maza to jab hai ki girton ko thaam le saqi

Jo badakash the purane vo uthte jaaten hain
Kahin se aab-e-baqa-e-dwam le saqi

Kati hai raat to hungama-gustari mein teri
Sehar qarib hai allah ka naam le saqi

---

1. अमृत 2. हंगामा फैलाने में

Saqi ساقی

To intoxicate somebody and then to see him fall
is quite easy
But the beauty lies in giving support to a falling
man, O Saqi

The drinkers of the old school are passing
away already
Procure from somewhere some elixir now, O Saqi

Your night has passed in the turmoil of the
bed verily
The dawn is approaching now, remember God,
O Saqi.

सरमाया व मेहनत

बंदा-ए-मजबूर को जाकर मेरा पैग़ाम दे
ख़िज़्र का पैग़ाम क्या है, यह पयाम-ए-क़ायनात

ऐ कि तुझको खा गया सरमायादारे-हीलागर[1]
शाख़े-आहू[2] पर रही सदियों तलक तेरी बरात

कट मरा नादां ख़याली देवताओं के लिए
सुक्र[3] की लज़्ज़त में तू लुटवा गया नक्दे-हयात[4]

मक्र की चालों से बाज़ी ले गया सरमायादार
इन्तिहा-ए-सादगी में खा गया मज़दूर मात

→

Banda-e-majboor ko jaakar mera paigham de
khizr ka paigham kya hai, yeh payam-e-kayanaat

Ae ki tujhko kha gaya sarmayadaar-e-heelagar
shaakh-e-aahoo per rahi sadiyon talak teri baraat

Kat mara naadaan khayali devtaon ke liye
sukr ki lazzat mein tu lutwa gaya naqd-e-hayat

Makr ki chaalon se baazi le gaya sarmayadaar
intiha-e-saadgi mein kha gaya mazdoor maat

1. बहाने बनाकर लूटने वाला पूंजीपति 2. दोषपूर्ण शाखा 3. नशे 4. जीवन की पूंजी

Capital and Labour

Go, and give my message to the workingman
Tell him, this message from Khizar is a life-giving message:

O you have been fleeced by the wily Capitalist
For centuries, you have remained caught in a fatalistic web

O you ignorant one, you sacrificed your life for imaginary gods
And under the effect of sporafic drug lost your life's wealth;

With his fraudulent practices, the capitalist has got the better of you
All because of your extreme simplicity, have you lost!

→

उठ कि अब बज़्मे-जहां का और ही अंदाज़ है
मशरिक़-ओ-मग़रिब में तेरे दौर का आग़ाज़ है

आफ़ताब-ए-ताज़ा[1] *पैदा बतन-ए-गेती*[2] *से हुआ*
आस्मां! डूबे हुए तारों का मातम कब तलक

तोड़ डाली फ़ितरत-ए-इन्सां ने ज़ंजीरें तमाम
दूरी-ए-जन्नत से रोती चश्म-ए-आदम कब तलक

Uth ki ab bazm-e-jahan ka aur hi andaaz hai
mashriq-o-maghrib mein tere daur ka aaghaaz hai

Aaftaab-taaza paida batne-gati se hua
aasmaan ! doobe húe taaron ka maatam kab talak

Tor daali fitrat-e-insaan ne zanjeerein tamaam
doori-e-jannat se roti chashm-e-Adam kab talak

---

1. नया सूरज 2. संसार की कोख

Arise, the world is in a different mood now
And the era that begins in east and west belongs to you.

A new sun is born from the womb of the earth
How long, O heaven, will you grieve for the stars that have set?

All shackles has human nature broken
How long could man live away from heaven!

हुनरवाने हिंद

इश्क़-ओ-ए-मस्ती का जनाज़ा है तखैयुल इनका
इनके अन्देशा-ए-तारीक में कौमों के मज़ार

मौत की नक़्शगरी इन के सनमख़ानों में
ज़िंदगी से हुनर इन बरहनों का बेज़ार

चश्म-ए आदम से छुपाते हैं मक़ामात-ए-बुलंद
करते है रूह को ख़्वाबीदा, बदन को बेदार

हिंद के शायरों, सूरतगरों, अफसानानवीस
आह बेचारों के अहसाब पे औरत है सवार

Ishqo-masti ka janaaza hai takheyul inka
inke andesha-e-tareek mein kaumon ke mazaar

Maut ki naqshgari inke sanamkhanon mein
zindagi se hunar in berhanon ka bezaar

Chashm-e-aadam se chhupate hain maqamaat-e-buland
karte hain rooh ko khawabida, badan ko bedaar

Hind ke shayaron, suratgaron, afsananavees
aah becharon ke ahsaab pe aurat hai sawar

The Artists of India

Their fancy is a funeral procession of romance
and passion
Their bleak heart, the burial ground of nations

They paint pictures of death, and display
Life, from their art, is far, far away

They show not the lofty spot to the human eye
The spirit, they send to sleep, and rouse the body
What a pity

On the very being
Of the poets, painters and fiction writers of India
Women have total suzrenity!

एक आरज़ू

दुनिया की महफ़िलों से उकता गया हूं या रब!
क्या लुत्फ़ अंजुमन का जब दिल ही बुझ गया हो

शोरिश[1] से भागता हूँ, दिल ढूंढता है मेरा
ऐसा सकूत[2] जिस पर तक़रीर भी फ़िदा हो

मरता हूं ख़ामशी[3] पर, ये आरज़ू है मेरी
दामन में कोह[4] के इक छोटा-सा झोंपड़ा हो

आज़ाद फ़िक्र से हूं, उज़लत में दिन गुज़ारूं
दुनिया के ग़म का दिल से कांटा निकल गया हो

लज़्ज़त सरोद की हो चिड़ियों के चहचहों में
चश्मों की शोरिशों में बाजा-सा बज रहा हो

Duniya ki mehfilon se ukta gaya hun ya rab
kya lutf anjuman ka jab dil hi bujh gaya ho

Shorish se bhagta hun, dil dhoondhta hai mera
aisa sakoot jis per taqreer bhi fida ho

Marta hoon khamshi per, ye aarzoo hai meri
daaman mein koh ke ik chhota-sa jhonpara ho

Azaad fikr se hoon, uzlat mein din guzarun
duniya ke gham ka dil se kanta nikal gaya ho

Lazzat sarod ki ho chiriyon ke chehchahon mein
chashmon ki shorishon mein baaja-sa baj raha ho

→

1. कोलाहल 2. चुप्पी 3. खामोशी 4. पहाड़

A Wish

I am sick and tired of the world around
What do I do of it, O Lord, when the heart is not in it!

I flee from noise and seek silence, more eloquent than speech
And a quiet hut by the hill-side need;

I wish, I were free from the cares of the world, have no sorrow
And live in peace;

Would that around my hut the birds sing and cataracts fall
And fill the atmosphere with mixed melody,

→

हो हाथ का सिरहाना, सब्ज़ा[1] का हो बिछौना
शरमाए जिससे जलवत ख़लवत में वो अदा हो

मानूस[2] इस क़दर हो सूरत से मेरी बुलबुल
नन्हें से दिल में उसके खटका न कुछ मेरा हो

सफ़ बांधे दोनों जानिब बूटे हरे-हरे हों
नद्दी का साफ़ पानी तस्वीर ले रहा हो

हो दिल-फ़रेब ऐसा कुहसार का नज़ारा
पानी भी मौज बनकर उठ-उठके देखता हो

→

Gul ki kali chatak kar paigham de kisi ka
Saghar zara-sa goya mujhko jahan numa ho

Ho hath ka sirhana, sabza ka ho bichhona
sharmae jisse jalvat khalvat mein woh ada ho

Manoos is qadar ho surat se meri bulbul
nanhen se dil mein uske khatka na kuchh mera ho

Saf baandhe dono jaanib boote hare-hare hon
naddi ka saaf pani tasveer le raha ho

Ho dil-fareb aisa kuhsaar ka nazara
pani bhi mauj bankar uth-uthke dekhta ho

---

1. हरियाली 2. परिचित

Let my arm be my pillow and greenery, my bed,
The nightingale should be so familiar with
my presence

That it should be free from all human fear,

On both sides of the hut, there should be a row
of trees
And a mirror like river should flow beside,

The sight of the hillside should be such that the
waters of the river
Rise in waves to see its beauty,

→

आग़ोश में ज़मीं की सोया हुआ हो सब्ज़ा
फिर-फिरके झाड़ियों में पानी चमक रहा हो

पानी को छू रही हो झुक-झुक के गुल की टहनी
जैसे हसीन कोई आईना देखता हो

मेहंदी लगाए सूरज जब शाम की दुल्हन को
सुर्ख़ी लिए सुनहरी हर फूल की क़बा हो

रातों को चलने वाले रह जाएं थक के जिस दम
उम्मीद उनकी मेरा टूटा हुआ दिया हो

बिजली चमक के उनको कुटिया मेरी दिखा दे
जब आसमां पे हर-सू बादल घिरा हुआ हो

→

Aaghosh mein zameen ki soya hua ho sabza
phir-phirke jhariyon mein pani chamak raha ho

Pani ko chhu rahi ho jhuk-jhuk ke gul ki tehni
jaise haseen koi aaina dekhata ho

Mehandi lagaye suraj jab sham ki dulhan ko
surkhi liye sunhari her phool ki qaba ho

Raaton ko chalne wale reh jaayen thak ke jis dam
ummeed unki mera toota hua diya ho

Bijli chamak ke unko kutiya meri dikha de
jab aasmaan pe her-su baadal ghira hua ho

There, should I have greenery all around
And water meandering through the bushes,

The rose-bough should bend and reach the
river water
Like a beautiful woman looking her face in
the mirror.

At the sunset, when the horizon glows red
The flowers should be wearing red and gold attire;

If some traveller at night feels tired
May my hut provide him succour

And the flash of lightning in the overcast sky
Lead him there.

→

पिछले पहर की कोयल, वो सुबह की मुअज़्ज़िन
मैं उसका हमनवा हूं, वो मेरी हमनवा हो

कानों पे हो न मेरे दैरा-ओ-हरम का अहसां
रौज़न[1] ही झोंपड़ी का मुझको सहरनुमा हो

फूलों को आए जिस दम शबनम वुज़ू कराने
रोना मेरा वुज़ू हो, नाला मेरा दुआ हो

इस ख़ामशी में जाएं इतने बुलन्द नाले
तारों के क़ाफ़िले को मेरी सदा दिरा[2] हो

हर दर्दमन्द दिल को रोना मेरा रुला दे
बेहोश जो पड़े हैं शायद उन्हें जगा दे

Pichhle pehar ki koyal, woh subah ki muazzin
main uska humnava hun, woh meri humnava ho

Kanon pe ho na mere dairo-harum ka ahsaan
rauzan hi jhonpari ka mujhko seharnuma ho

Phoolon ko aaye jis dam shabnam vuzoo karane
rona mera vuzoo ho, naala mere dua ho

Is khamshi mein jaayen itne buland naale
taaron ke qafile ko meri sada dira ho

Her dardmand dil ko rona mera rula de
behosh jo pare hain shayad unhen jaga de

---

1. खिड़की 2. घड़ियाल की आवाज़

The cuckoo at dawn should wake me up
And with each other we should converse,

The window in my hut should herald the dawn
And no outside agency on me have sway,

When the dew-drops fall and bathe the flowers
I should with tears cleanse myself and cry in prayer

The cry should pierce the sky
And to the stars, it should sound like a gong

Let my cry move every feeling heart
O may it also wake up the slumbering lot!

पंजाब के दहक़ान से

बता क्या तेरी ज़िंदगी का है राज़
हज़ारों बरस से तू है ख़ाकबाज़

इसी ख़ाक में दब गयी तेरी आग
सहर की अज़ां हो गयी, अब तो जाग

ज़मीं में है गो ख़ाकियों की बरात
नहीं इस अंधेरे में आब-ए-हयात

ज़माने में झूठा है उसका नगीं
जो अपनी .ख़ुदी को परखता नहीं

निशाने-शउ.िबो-कबाइल को तोड़
रसूमें कुहन के सलासल को तोड़

यही दीन-ए-मोहकम यही फतह-ए-बाब
कि दुनिया में तौहीद हो बेहिजाब

Bata kya teri zindhgi ka hai raaz
hazaron baras se tu hai khaakbaaz

Isee khaak mein dab gayee teri aag
sehar ki azaan ho gayee, ab to jaag

Zamin mein hai go khakiyon ki baraat
nahin is andhere mein aab-e-hayat

Zamane mein jhutha hai uska nageen
jo apni khudi ko parakhta nahin

Nishane-shaobo-kabaiel ko tor
rasume kuhan ke salasal ko tor

Yahi deen-e-mohkam yahi fatw-e-baab
ki duniya mein toheed ho behijaab

To the Peasants of Punjab

How have you survived, tell me;
You have been trampled to dust for thousands
of years

And under the earth lies buried your native fire,
Call for the morning prayer has gone out, wake
up now.

You may draw your bread from underneath the
soil though
The elixer of life cannot be in darkness found

He who does not cultivate strength
Never realizes what he deserves;

Break the shackles of customs obsolete,
Unity of faith and one universal God—
Herein lies your redemption, your sweet triumph.

लाला-ए-सहरा[1]

यह गुंबद-ए-मीनाई[2]*, यह आलम-ए-तनहाई*
मुझको तो डराती है इस दश्त की पहनाई

भटका हुआ राही मैं, भटका हुआ राही तू
मंज़िल है कहां तेरी ऐ लाला-ए-सहराई

तू शाख़ से क्यों फूटा, मैं शाख़ से क्यों टूटा
एक जज़्बा-ए-पैदाई, इक लज़्ज़ते-यकताई[3]

उस मौज के मातम में रोती है भंवर की आंख
दरिया से उठी लेकिन साहिल से न टकराई

है गर्मी-ए-आदम से हंगामा-ए-आलम गर्म
सूरज भी तमाशाई, तारे भी तमाशाई

ऐ बाद-ए-बयाबानी मुझको भी इनायत हो
ख़ामोशी-ओ-दिल सोज़ी, सरमस्ती-ओ-रानाई

Yeh gumbade-meenai, yeh aalme-tanhaai
mujhko to darati hai is dasht ki pehnaai

Bhatka hua raahi main, bhatka hua raahi tu
manzil he kahan teri ae lala-e-sehrai

Tu shaakh se kyon phuta, main shaakh se kyon toota
ik jazba-e-paidaai, ik lazzat-e-yaktaai

Us mauj ke maatam mein roti hai bhanwar ki aankh
dariya se uthee lekin sahil se na takraai

Hai garmi-e-aadam se hangama-e-aalam garm
suraj bhi tamashaai, taare bhi tamashaai

Ae baad-e-bayabani mujhko bhi inaayat ho
Khamoshi-o-dil sozi sar masti-o- ranai

---

1. मरुस्थल का फूल 2. आकाश का गुंबद 3. अनुपमता का आनंद

The Tulip of the Desert

The dome of the sky, this lonely expanse,
This vastness of the desert frightens me

Like you, I too have my way lost,
What is your goal, O let me know?

Why did you sprout on the branch, why was I plucked
from the bough?
Perhaps it is the desire to unfold, the desire to
be unique;

The whirlpool mourns for the wave
That rose from the ocean but reached not the shore

It is only owing to the hot blood of man that the
pulse of the universe beats
While the sun and moon merely look on

O cool breeze of the desert let me also partake of,
however slight
Your heart's warmth, your glory, your silence
and delight.

हिमालय से

ऐ हिमालय, ऐ फ़सीले किश्वरे हिंदोस्ताँ
चूमता है तेरी पेशानी को झुक के आसमां

तुझमें कुछ पैदा नहीं देरीना-रोज़ी के निशां
तू जवां है गर्दिश-ए-शामो-सहर के दरमियाँ

एक जलवा था कलीम-ए-तूर सीना के लिये
तू तजल्ली है सरापा चश्म-ए-बीना के लिये

इम्तिहान-ए दीदा-ए-ज़ाहिर में कोहिस्तां है तू
पासबां अपना है तू दीवार-ए-हिंदोस्तां है तू

मतला-ए-अव्वल फ़लक जिसका हो वो दीवां है तू
सूए खिलवत गाहे दिल दामन-कश-ए इंसां है तू

बर्फ़ ने बांधी है दस्तारे-फज़ीलत तेरे सर
खंदाज़न है जो कुलाहे मेहरे आलम ताब पर

→

Ae himalaya, ae fasiley kishwarey hindostan
chumta hai teri peshani ko jhuk ke aasmaan

tujhme kuchh paida nahin derina-rozi ke nishan
tu jawan hai gardish-e-shaam-o-sehar ke darmiyan

Ek jalwa tha kalim-e-toor seena ke liye
tu tajalli hai sarapa chashm-e-beena ke liye

Imtihan-e_deeda-e zaahir mein kohistan hai tu
paaswan apna hai tu deewar-e-hindostan hai tu

matla avval falak jiska ho woh deewan hai tu
sue khilwat gaahe dil daaman-kash-e-insaan hai tu

Barf ne baandhi hai dastaare-fazilat tere sar
khandazan hai jo kulahe mehre aalam taap per

To Himalaya

O Himalaya, the bastion of our nation,
The very heaven bends to kiss your brow;

Untouched by the passage of centuries in time's diurnal motion
Even now youthful as ever you glow

While Moses had to go to mount Sinai for a radiant sight
For men of vision, you are a minaret bright

An ordinary mountain to the common eye
Our protector, you are for us a rampart

Beckoning man to solitude and seclusion
You are the poetic collection whose opening verse is heaven

Snow has tied a turban of honour on your head
Which far outrivals the tiara of the sun

→

तेरी उम्र-ए-रफ़्ता की इक आन है अहद-ए-कुहन
वादियों में है तेरी काली घटाएं ख़ेमाज़न

चोटियां तेरी सुरैया से हैं सरगर्म-ए-सुख़न
तू ज़मीं पर और पहनाए-फ़लक तेरा वतन

ऐ हिमालय दास्तां उस वक़्त की कोई सुना
मस्कन-ए-आबाए-इनसां जब बना दामन तेरा

कुछ बता उस सीधी-सादी ज़िंदगी का माजरा
दाग़ जिस पर ग़ाज़ा-ए-रंग-ए-तकल्लुफ़ का न था

हां दिखा दे ऐ तसव्वुर फिर वो सुबह-ए-शाम तू
दौड़ पीछे की तरफ़ ऐ गर्दिश-ए-अय्याम तू

Teri umr-e-rafta ki ik aan hai ahad-e-kuhan
wadiyon mein hai teri kaali ghatayen khemazan

chotiyan teri suraiya se hain sargam-e sukhan
tu zameen per aur pehnae-falak tera vatan

Ae himalaya daastan us waqt ki koi suna
maskane aabaae-insaan jab bana daaman tera

kuchh bata us sidhi-saadi zindagi ka maajra
daagh jis per ghazaaye-rang-e-takalluf ka na tha

Haan dikha de ae tasavvur phir woh subeh-sham tu
daur pichhe ki taraf ae gardish-e-ayyaam tu

Past ages to you only glory lend
Your clouds have in the valley their settlement spun

Your peaks with constellation hold converse
Even though you are on earth situated, your home is heaven

Himalaya, tell us some tale from the times past
When our ancestors in caverns lived,

Tell us of that life simple and plain by formalities unstained

O imagination, once again those morns and evening show
And take us to the ages long ago.

ज़ोह्द[1] और रिंदी[2]

इक मौलवी साहब की सुनाता हूँ कहानी
तेज़ी नहीं मंज़ूर तबीयत की दिखानी।

शोहरा था बहुत आपकी सूफ़ी-मनिशी[3] का
करते थे अदब उनका अआली-व-अदानी[4]

कहते थे कि पिनहाँ है तसव्वुफ़[5] में शरीयत[6]
जिस तरह कि अल्फ़ाज में मुज़मर[7] हो मआनी[8]

लबरेज़ मय-ए-ज़ोहद से थी दिल की सुराही
थी तह में कहीं दुर्द-ए-ख़्याल-ए-हमादानी[9]।

करते थे बयाँ आप करामात का अपनी
मंज़ूर थी तादाद मुरीदों की बढ़ानी

→

Ik maulavi sahab ki sunata hun kahani
tezi nahin manzoor tabiyat ki dikhani

shohra tha bahut aapki sufi-manishi ka
karte the abad unka aali-ve-adaani

kehate the ki pinhaan hai tasavvuf mein shariyat
jis tarah ki alfaaz mein muzmar ho maani

labrez may-e-zohad se thi dil ki surahi
thi teh mein kahin durd-e-khayal-e-hamadani

karte the bayaan aap karamaat ka apni
manzjoor thi tadaad muridon ki badhani

---

1. भक्ति 2. चरित्रहीनता शराबीपन 3. भक्ति 4. छोटे-बड़े 5. सूफीवाद 6. इस्लाम का धर्मशास्त्र 7. निहित 8. अर्थ 9. सर्वज्ञता की भ्रांति

Piety and Profligacy

I am going to tell you the story of a Maulvi
But pray, think not that I do it to show my intelligence off;

For his mystical disposition the Maulvi had earned renown
And was held in great esteem by the young and old alike

He held that Shariat is wrapped in mysticism
As meaning in words,

With wine of piety his heart was full to the brim
But at the bottom somewhere lay the conceit of omniscience there

And in order to increase the number of followers
He loved to narrate, his achievements great

→

मुद्दत से रहा करते थे हमसाय में मेरे
थी रिंद से ज़ाहिद की मुलाक़ात पुरानी

हज़रत ने मिरे एक शनासा से यह पूछा
इक़बाल! कि है कुमरी-ए-शमशादे[10] मआनी

पाबन्दी-ए-अहकाम-ए-शरीयत में ये कैसा
गो शेर में है रश्क-ए-कलाम-ए हमादानी

सुनता हूँ कि काफ़िर नहीं हिन्दू को समझता
है ऐसा अक़ीदा, असर-ए-फ़ल्सफ़ा-दानी

है इसकी तबीयत में तशय्यो भी ज़रा सा
तफ़ज़ीले-अली हमने सुनी उसकी ज़बानी

→

muddat se raha karte the humsaye mein mere
thi rind se zaahid ki mulakat purani

hazrat ne mirey ek shanasa se ye puchha
Iqbal ! ki hai kumri-e-shamshade maani

pabandi-e-ahkaam-e-shariyat mein hai kaisa
go sher mein hai rashk-e-kalam-e hamadani

sunta hoon ki kafir nahin hindu ko samajhta
hai aisa aqida, asr-e-falsafa-daani

hai iski tabiyat mein tashayyo bhi zara sa
tafzeele-ali humne suni uski zabani

---

1. बुलबुल यानी कवि

This pious man had been my neighbour for a
long time
And had been acquainted with this profligate
quite a while

One day he asked a friend of mine
"This Iqbal who seems to be knowing the meaning
of things

Is he particular in following the Sheriat too?
Though in poetry he should be envy of Kalim Hamdani
himself

I hear he doesn't consider Hindus, infidels
Is it because of the influence of philosophy?

Aren't there traces of Shiaism too in him?
I have myself heard him praising Ali

→

समझा है कि है राग इबादात में दाख़िल
मक़सूद है मज़हब की मगर ख़ाक उड़ानी

कुछ आर[1] उसे हुस्न-फ़रोशों से नहीं है
आदत यह हमारे शोअरा की है पुरानी

गाना है जो शब को तो सहर को है तिलावत
इस रम्ज़[2] के अब तक न खुले हम पे मआनी

लेकिन यह सुना अपने मुरीदों से है मैंने
बेदाग़ है मानंदे-सहर उसकी जवानी

मजमूआ-ए-अज़दाद है इक़बाल नहीं है
दिल दफ्तर-ए-हिकमत है तबीयत ख़फक़ानी[3]

→

Samjha hai ki hai raag ibadaat mein dakhil
maqsood hai mazhab ki magar khaaq urani

Kuchh aar use husn-faroshon se nahin hai
aadat yeh humare shoara ki hai purani

Gana hai jo shab ko to sehar ko hai tilavat
is ramz ke ab tak na khule hum pe meani

Lekin yeh suna apne muridon se hai maine
bedaagh hai manand-e-sehar uski jawani

majmua-e-azdaad hai Iqbal nahin hai
dil daftar-e-hikmat hai tabiyat khafqaani

---

1. शर्म 2. रहस्य 3. सौदाई

His purpose seems to be to malign religion
He doesn't mind being with the prostitutes even,

He goes to the singing girls at night and recites the
Quran in the morning
For ages these poets have behaved like this
I don't understand this man

And I have heard this too, from my followers
That his youth is pure like the fresh dawn,

Don't you think that this man is bundle of
contradictions
Wise and confused at the same time

→

रिंदी से भी आगाह, शरीयत से भी वाक़िफ़
पूछो जो तसव्वुफ़ की तो मंसूर का सानी

इस शख़्स की हम पर तो हक़ीक़त नहीं खुलती,
होगा यह किसी और ही इसलाम का बानी

अलक़िस्सा बहुत तूल दिया वअज़ को अपने,
ता देर रही आपकी यह नग्ज़-बयानी[1]

इस शहर में जो बात हो उड़ जाती है सब में,
मैंने भी सुनी अपने अहिब्बा की ज़बानी

इक दिन जो सरे-राह मिले हज़रत-ए-ज़ाहिद,
फिर छिड़ गई बातों में वही बात पुरानी

फ़रमाया, शिकायत वो मुहब्बत के सबब थी,
था फ़र्ज़ मिरा राह शरीयत की दिखानी

→

Rindi se bhi aagaah, shariyat se bhi waqif
puchho jo tasavvuf ki to mansoor ka saani

Is shakhs ki hum per to haqiqat nahin khulti
hoga yeh kisi aur hi islaam ka baani

Alkissa bahut tool diya váz ko apne
taader rahi aapki yeh nagz-bayani

Is shehar mein jo baat ho ur jaati hai sab mein
maine bhi suni apne ahibba ki zabani

Ik din jo sarey-raah miley hazrate-zaahid
phir chhir gayee baaton mein wahi baat purani

Farmaya shikayat wo muhabbat ke sabab thi
tha farz mira raah shariyat ki dikhani

---

1. भाषणबाज़ी

At once given to profligacy and the path of Islam
In mysticism, he is an equal of Mansoor

I'm unable to fathom this man
Perhaps he wants to found some other brand of Islam!

So he went on with his oration a long while
Emphasising it over much

Every word takes wings in this city
And I too heard the account from my friends

And one day, I ran into the man myself
And the story came up again.

He said that he was complaining because he loved me
And that it was his duty to show me the path of true Islam.

→

मैंने ये कहा कोई गिला मुझको नहीं है,
यह आपका हक़ था ज़रहे-कुर्ब-ए-मकानी [1]

ख़म है सर-ए-तसलीम मिरा आपके आगे,
पीरी है तवाज़े के सबब मेरी जवानी

गर आपको मालूम नहीं मेरी हक़ीकत
पैदा नहीं कुछ इससे क़सूर-ए-हमादानी

मैं ख़ुद भी नहीं अपनी हक़ीक़त का शुनासा
गहरा है मिरे बहर-ए-खयालात का पानी

मुझको भी तमन्ना है कि इक़बाल को देखूँ,
की उसकी जुदाई में बहुत अश्क-फ़िशानी

इक़बाल भी इक़बाल से आगाह नहीं है,
कुछ इसमें तमस्ख़ुर [2] *नहीं वल्लाह नहीं है*

Maine ye kaha koi gila mujhko nahin hai
yeh aapka huq tha zarhe-kurbe-makani

Kham hai sarey-tasleem mira aapke aagey
peeri hai tavaazo ke sabab meri jawani

Gar aapko maloom nahin meri haqiqat
paida nahin kuchh isse qasure-hamadaani

Main khud bhi nahin apni haqiqat ka shunaasa
gehara hai mire beharey-khayalaat ka paani

Mujhko tamanna hai ki Iqbal ko dekhun
ki uski judaai mein bahut ashq-fishani

Iqbal bhi Iqbal se aagaah nahin hai
kuchh ismein tamaskhur nahin vallaah nahin hai

---

1. पड़ोस के कारण 3. मज़ाक़

I said, "I don't mind at all"
It is your right, living as you do so near me

I bow my head before you with regard,
Your age deserves all the reverence from my youth.

If you don't understand me, it is none of your faults
I myself don't understand what I am!

The ocean of my thought is too deep to fathom even for me,

I am day and night yearning to meet real Iqbal,
Sundered from him I have filled an ocean with tears

Even Iqbal is not familiar with Iqbal!
It is no joke at all, sir, none at all

जावेद के नाम

(लंदन में उसका पहला खत आने पर)

दयारे-इश्क़ में अपना मक़ाम पैदा कर
नया ज़माना है नये सुबह-शाम पैदा कर

खुदा अगर दिल-ए-फितरत-शनास दे तुझको
संकूत-ए-लाला-ओ-गुल से कलाम पैदा कर

उठा न शीशा-गराने फरंग का अहसान
सफ़ाले-हिंद से मीना-ओ-जाम पैदा कर

मैं शाख़नाक हूं मेरी ग़ज़ल है मेरा समर
मेरे समर से मये लालाफ़ाम पैदा कर

मेरा तरीक़ा अमीरी नहीं फ़कीरी है
खुदी न बेच ग़रीबी में नाम पैदा कर

Dayaare-ishq mein apna maqaam paida kar
naya zamana hai naye subeh-shaam paida kar

Khuda agar dil-e-fitrat-shanaas de tujhko
sakut-e-laala-o-gul se kalaam paida kar

Utha na sheesha-garaney farang ka ahsaan
safaley-hind se meena-o-jaam paida kar

Main shaakhnaak hun meri ghazal hai mera samar
mere samar se maye laalafaam paida kar

Mera tarika ameeri nahin faqiri hai
khudi ne bech gharibi mein naam paida kar

To Javed

(On receiving his first letter in London)

Make your place in the realms of love
In this new age, your own morning, your own evening create

May God bless you with the love of nature
May you with the tulips a silent communion relish;

Do not be dazzled by the glamour of the West
With the clay of India instead your goblet make;

I am a vineyard, my ghazal is my fruit
From this fruit, let you produce ruby colured wine;

My ways are not the ways of the rich, I am a mendicant, in fact
Make a name even in poverty, preserve your self-respect

हम बग़ल दरिया से है ऐ क़तरा-ए-बेताब तू
पहले गौहर था, बना अब गौहर-ए-नायाब तू

आह! खोला किस अदा से तूने राज़-ए-रंगो-ए-बू
मैं अभी तक हूँ असीर-ए-इम्तियाज़-ए-रंगो-ओ-बू

मिट के ग़ोग़ा[1] ज़िंदगी का शोरिश-ए-महशर बना
यह शरारा बुझ के आतिश-खाना-ए-आज़र बना

नफ़्से-हस्ती[2] इक करिश्मा है दिल-आगाह का
"ला" के दरिया में निहां मोती है "इलल्लाह" का

चश्म-ए-नाबीना से मख़्फ़ी मानी-ए-अंजाम है
थम गई जिस दम तड़प, सीमाब सीमे-ख़ाम है

Hum bagal dariya se hai ae qatra-e-betaab tu
pehle gauhar tha, bana ab gaurhar-e-nayaab tu

Aah ! khola kis ada se tune raaz-e-rang-o-bu
main abhi tak hoon aseer-e-imtiyaaz-e-rango-bu

Mit ke ghogha zindagi ka shorish-e-mehshar bana
yeh sharara bujh ke aataih-khana-e-aazar bana

Nafs-e-hasti ik karishma he dil-aagaah ka
'la' ke dariya mein nihaan bhauti hai 'Ilallaah ka

Chashm-e-nabeena se makhfi maani-e-anjaam hai
tham gayee jis dam tarap, seemaab seeme-khaam hai

---

1. शोर 2. जीवन-तत्व

Swami Ramtirth

You are its restless drop while we are only clinging
· to the ocean

A jewel earlier, now you have become a ruby rare
With rare insight you have revealed truth, and its
oneness shown

While we are still in the kaleidoscope caught
Rejecting the cacophony of the world you have heard
the divine call

A spark you are, which, extinguished to the world,
Has turned you into a temple fire,
In negation, affirmation

And in the extinction of the self, the magic of
divinity lies,
The end of man is hidden from the unseeing eyes.

शेक्सपीयर

शफ़क़-ए-सुबह को दरिया का ख़राम आईना
नग़मा-ए-शाम को खामोशी-ए-शाम आईना

बर्ग-ए-गुल आईना आरिज़-ए-ज़ेबाए बहार
शाहिद-ए मय के लिये हुजलाए जाम आईना

है तेरे फ़िकरे-फलक रस से कमाल-ए-हस्ती
क्या तेरी फितरत-ए रोशन थी मआल-ए-हस्ती

तुझको जब दीदाए-दीदार-ए-तलब ने ढूंढा
ताब-ए खुरशीद में खुरशीद को पिन्हा देखा

चश्म-ए-आलम से तो हस्ती रही मस्तूर तेरी
और आलम को तेरी आंख ने उरियां देखा

हफज़-ए-असरार का फितरत को है सौदा ऐसा
राज़दां फिर न करेगी कोई पैदा ऐसा

Shafq-e-subah ko dariya ka kharaam aaina
naghma-e-shaam ko khamoshi-e-shaam aaina

Barg-e-gul ko aaina aareeze-zebaae bahaar
shahid-e-mai ki liye hujlaye jaam aaina

Hai tere fikr-e-falak ras se kamaal-e-hasti
kya teri fitrat-e roshan thi maale-hasti

Tujhko jab didaae-didaar-e-talab ne dhoondha
taab-e-khursheed mein khursheed ko pinha dekha

Chashm-e-aalam se to hasti rahi mastoor teri
aur aalam ko teri aankha ne uriyaan dekha

hafz-e-asraar ka fitrat ko hai sauda aisa
razdaan phir na karegi koi paida aisa

Shakespeare

The flow of the river reflects the glow of dawn
And the song of the evening is reflected in its silence,

The loveliness of spring is in a rose-petal reflected,
And the beauty of the wine is reflected in its Chalice;

As beauty mirrors truth and heart mirrors beauty
Life of man finds its finest reflection in your shy-
soaring imagination.

Was your mind the ultimate in human brilliance?
When the searching eye looked out for you
It found the sun under its own brilliance;

From the eye of the world, you remained
hidden though
Your eye saw the world in its entirety even so

Nature, which guards its secrets so well
Will never produce another who can its secrets
so well tell

बच्चों के लिए (बच्चे की दुआ)

लब पे आती है दुआ बनके तमन्ना मेरी
ज़िन्दगी शम्मअ की सूरत हो खुदाया मेरी

दूर दुनिया का मेरे दम से अंधेरा हो जाए
हर जगह मेरे चमकने से उजाला हो जाए

हो मेरे दम से यूंही मेरे वतन की ज़ीनत
जिस तरह फूल से होती है चमन की ज़ीनत

ज़िन्दगी हो मेरी परवाने की सूरत या रब
इल्म की शम्मअ से हो मुझको मोहब्बत या रब

हो मेरा काम ग़रीबों की हिमायत करना
दर्द-मन्दों से, ज़ईफ़ों[1] से मोहब्बत करना

मेरे अल्लाह! बुराई-से बचाना मुझको
नेक जो राह हो उस रह पे चलाना मुझको

Lab pe aati hai dua banke tamanna meri
zindagi shammá ki surat ho khudaya meri

door duniya ka mere dam se andhera ho jaaye
her jagah mere chamakne se ujaala ho jaaye

Ho mere dam se yunhi mere vatan ki zeenat
jis tarah phool se hoti hai chaman ki zeenat

Zindgi ho meri parvane ki surat yaa Rab
Ilm ki shammá se ho mujhko mohabbat ya Rab

ho mera kaam garibon ki himayat karna
dard-mandon se, zaifon se mohabbat karna

Mere Allah ! burai se bachana mujhko
nek jo rah ho us raah pe chalana mujhko

---

1. बुजुर्गों

Children's Prayer

In the form of a prayer, it is my desire O God
Let my life be like a candle that burns for others

Let there be light wherever I go
May that place never darkness know

Like the flower that lends charm to the garden
Let me bring glory to my nation

Let my life be like that of the moth
Let me be a lover of knowledge, O lord

Let me be on the side of the poor always
And a supporter of the weak and the feeble

Let me follow the righteous path
Save me from evil always, my Lord!

गुले-पज़मुर्दा

किस ज़बां से ऐ गुल-ए-पज़मुर्दा[1] तुझ को गुल कहूं
किस तरह तुझको तमन्ना-ए-दिले बुलबुल कहूं

थी कभी मौज-ए-सबा गेहवारा-ए-जुम्बां[2] तिरा
नाम था सेहन-ए-गुलिस्तां में गुल-ए-खंदां तिरा

तेरे एहसां का नसीम-ए सुबह को इक़रार था
बाग़ तेरे दम से गोया तबला-ए-अत्तार[3] था

तुझ पे बरसाता है शबनम दीदा-ए-गिरयाँ मिरा
है निहां तेरी उदासी में दिल-ए-वीरां मिरा

मेरी बरबादी की है छोटी-सी इक तस्वीर तू
.ख्वाब मेरी ज़िंदगी थी जिसकी है ताबीर तू

Kis zabaan se ae gul-e-pazmurda tujhko gul kahun
kis tarah tujhko tamanna-e-dil-e bulbul kahun

thi kabhi moje-saba gehawara-e-jumbaan tira
naam tha sehan-e-gulistaan mein gul-e-khandaan tira

Tere ahsaan ka naseem-e subah ko iqraar tha
baagh tere dam se goya tabla-e-attaar tha

Tujh pe barsaata hai shabnam deeda-e-giryaan mira
hai nihaan teri udasi mein dil-e-veeraan mira

meri barbaadi ki hai chhoti-si ik tasveer tu
khawab meri zindgi thi jiski hai tabeer tu

1. मुरझाया हुआ फूल 2. झूलता हुआ पंगूरा 3. सुगंध-पात्र

The Withered Rose

How at all shall I call you a rose, O withered flower
How can I call you the goal of a nightingale's passion!

There was a time when the morning breeze cradled you in their arm
And you were known as the laughing flower in the garden

The morning breeze felt favoured by your presence.
And the garden overflowed with fragrance because of you

But now my eyes shed tears for you like drops of dew
And I see my own sorry state imaged forth in your plight-

You are in miniature my sorrowful lot
My life too was full of dreams, and their reality thou art.

दो सितारे

आये जो क़िरआं[1] में दो सितारे
कहने लगा एक दूसरे से

यह वस्ल मुदाम हो तो क्या ख़ूब
अंजामे-ख़राम हो तो क्या ख़ूब

थोड़ा सा जो मेहरबां फ़लक हो
हम दोनों की एक ही चमक हो

लेकिन यह विसाल की तमन्ना
पैग़ामे-फ़िराक़ थी सरापा

गर्दिश तारों का है मुक़द्दर
हर एक की राह है मुक़र्रर

है .ख्वाब सबाते-आशनाई[2]
आईन[3] जहां का है जुदाई

Aaye jo qiraan mein do sitare
kehne laga ek doosare se

yeh vasl mudaam ho to kya khoob
anjaam-kharame ho to kya khoob

Thora sa jo meharbaan falak ho
hum dono ki ek hi chamak ho

Lekin yeh visaal ki tamanna
paighame-firaq thin saraapa

gardishe taaron ka hai muqaddar
her ek ki raah hai muqarrar

Hai Khawab sabaate-aashnaai
aain jahaan ka hai judaai

---

1. बुर्ज 2. स्थायी मित्रता 3. नियम

Two Stars

Two stars said to each other as they came face
to face
How wonderful if our journey comes to an end here

How wonderful if our union becomes eternal;
Would that God be a little more kind

And our separate light is combined!
This desire for instant separation :

Mutability is the planet's destiny
And their orbit is set already

Eternal union is indeed a dream
And separation, nature's law supreme.

अपने शे'र से

है गिला मुझको तेरी लज़्ज़ते पैदाई का
तू हुआ फ़ाश तो हैं अब मरे असरार भी फ़ाश

शोले से टूट के मिस्ले-शरर आवारा न रह
कर किसी सीना-ए-पुरसोज़ में ख़िलवत की तलाश

Hai gila mujhko teri lazzate paidai ka
tu hua faash to hain ab mere asraar bhi faash

sholey se tootke mashle-e-sharar awara na rah
kar kisi seena-e-pursoz mein khilwat ki talash

To My Verse

You are so happy that you are created
You gloat, and know not what I really desire:

O find a solitary seat in some feeling heart
Rather than wandering like a spark sundered
from its fire

तन्हाई

तनहाई-ए-शब में है हज़ीं[1] क्या
अंजुम[2] नहीं तेरे हमनशीं क्या?

ये रफ़्त[3]-ए-आसमां ख़ामोश
.ख्वाबीदा ज़मीं, आसमां ख़ामोश

ये चांद, ये दश्तो-दर, ये कोहसार
फितरत है तमाम नस्तरीं ज़ार

मोती ख़ुशरंग प्यारे-प्यारे
यानी तेरे आंसुओं के तारे

किस शै की तुझे हवस है ऐ दिल
क़ुदरत तेरी हमनफस है ऐ दिल

Tanhai-e-shab mein hai hazim kya
anjum nahin tere humnashin kya?

Ye raft-e-aasmaane khamosh
khawabida zameen, aasmaan khamosh

Ye chand, ye dashto-dar, ye kohsaar
fitrat hai tamaam nastarin zaar

Moti khushrang pyare-pyare
yaani tere aansuon ke taare

Kis shai ki tujhe havas hai ae dil!
kudrat teri humnafas hai ae dil!

---

1. कमी 2. सितारे 3. ऊँचाई

Solitude

What is it that you lack in the solitude of night?
Don't you have the stars for company,

The silence of the high-vaulting sky
The dream-like beauty all around

The moon, the forest and the hill
And the white roses everywhere,

And lovely dew drops in your eyes
Like the stars in the sky?

What more do you want, O heart
When you and nature are each other's part?

एक शाम

(दरिया-ए नेकर के किनारे पर)

ख़ामोश है चांदनी क़मर की
शाखें हैं ख़मोश. हर शजर की

वादी के नवा-फ़रोश ख़ामोश
कोहसार के सब्ज़पोश ख़ामोश

फितरत बेहोश हो गयी है
आग़ोश में शब के सो गयी है

कुछ ऐसा सकूत का फ़सूं है
'नेकर' का ख़राम भी सुकूं है

→

Khamosh hai chandni qamar ki
shakhen hain khamosh her shajer ki

Vadi ke nava-farosh khamosh
kohsaar ke sabzposh khamosh

Fitrat behosh ho gayee hai
aaghosh mein shab ke so gayee hai

Kuchh aisa sakoot ka fasoon hai
nekar ka kharaam bhi sakoon hai

An Evening

(On the banks of river Necker [2])

The silent spread of the moon is quiet
And quiet are the branches of every tree.

The birds in the valley have gone silent all
And silent the greenery that wraps the hill, and
the field

In the lap of the night nature itself is fallen asleep—
The silence such a spell of magic casts

That the very flow of Necker only silence gives;
As a procession going without a sound

→

1. Heidelberg (Germany)

तारों का ख़मोश कारवां है
ये क़ाफ़िला बेदरा रवां है

ख़ामोश हैं कोहो-दश्तो-दरिया
क़ुदरत है मुराक़बे में गोया

ऐ दिल! तू भी खमोश हो जा
आग़ोश में ग़म को लेके सो जा

Taaron ka khamosh kaarwan
ye qafila bedara rawan hai

Khamosh hain koho-dashto-dariya
qudrat hai muraqabe mein goya

Ae dil! tu bhi khamosh ho ja
aaghosh mein ghum ko leke so ja

Constantly on the move
The caravan of the stars is silent

The river, the forest and the hill-are silent all
And silent all nature as if in contemplation deep—

O my heart, let you too be at peace
And with sorrow beside you, fall asleep.

शिकवा से

क्यों ज़ियांकार[1] बनूं, सूद-फ़रामोश रहूं
फ़िक्रे-फ़र्दा[2] न करूँ महवे-ग़मे-दोश[3] रहूँ

नाले बुलबुल के सुनूं और हमातनगोश रहूं
हमनवा मैं भी कोई गुल हूं, कि ख़ामोश रहूं

जुरअत-आमोज़[4] मिरी ताबे-सुख़न है मुझको
शिकवा अल्लाह से ख़ाकम-बदहन[5] है मुझको

है बजा-शेवा-ए-तस्लीम[6] में मशहूर हैं हम
क़िस्सा-ए-दर्द सुनाते हैं कि मजबूर हैं हम

साज़-ए-ख़ामोश हैं फ़रियाद से मामूर हैं हम
नाला आता है अगर लब पे तो माज़ूर हैं हम

ऐ ख़ुदा! शिकवा-ए-अरबाबे-वफ़ा भी सुन ले
ख़ूगरे-हम्द[7] से थोड़ा सा गिला भी सुन ले

→

Kyon Ziyaankar banoon, sood-faramosh rahoon
fikre-farda na karoon mehve-ghame-dosh rahoon

naale bulbul ke sunoon aur humatangosh rahoon
humnava main bhi koi gul hoon ki khamosh rahoon

Juráet-aamoz miri taabe-sukhan hai mujhko
shikva allaah se khakam-badhan hai mujhko

Hai baja-sheva-e-tasleem mein mashhoor hain hum
qissa-e-dard sunate hain ki majboor hain hum

saaze-khamosh hain fariyaad se mamoor hain hum
naala aata hai agar lab pe to majoor hain hum

Ae khuda shikva-e-arbaabe-wafa bhi sun le
khugare-hamd se thoda se gila bhi sun le

---

1. हानिकर 2. आने वाले कल की चिंता 3. बीते कल के विवाद में लीन 4. उत्साहजनक 5. मुंह में खाक 6. विनम्रता का चलन 7. प्रशंसा करने का आदी

Excerpts from Complaint

Why should I incur losses only and my gains
mind not
Why shouldn't I think of tomorrow

Why should I remain enveloped in yesterday's sorrow
Shall I merely listen to the plaintive notes of
the nightingale,
Am I a flower that should remain silent and never
tell its tale

It is my courage that lends meaning to my poetry
With my mouth filled with dust, O God I complain
to thee

It is true that we are known for our instinctive
devotion to you
We are telling our tale of sorrow because we are
compelled to

We may be silent instrument but we are full of grief
And expression is the only way we can hope to
get relief
We are used to singing your glories though
O God listen to our complaint too :

→

हम से पहले था अजब तेरे जहां का मंज़र
कहीं मस्जूद थे पत्थर, कहीं माबूद शजर

खूगरे-पैकरे-महसूस[1] थी इंसां की नज़र
मानता फ़िर कोई अनदेखे खुदा को क्योंकर

तुझ को मालूम है लेता था कोई नाम तिरा?
कुव्वते-बाज़ू-ए-मुस्लिम ने किया काम तिरा

बस रहे थे यहीं सलजूक़ भी तूरानी भी
अहले-चीं चीन में, ईरान में सासानी भी

इसी मामूरे में आबाद थे यूनानी भी
इसी दुनिया में यहूदी भी थे नसरानी भी

पर तिरे नाम पे तलवार उठाई किसने
बात जो बिगड़ी हुई थी, वह बनाई किसने

→

Hum se pehle tha ajab tere jahaan ka manzar
Kahin masjood the patthar, kahin mabood shajar

Khugare-paikare-mehsoos thi insaan ki nazar
Manta phir koi andekhe khuda ko kyonkar

Tujh ko maloom hai leta tha koi naam tira
Kuvvate-baazu-e-muslim ne kiya kaam tira

Bas rahe the yahin saljooq bhi turaani bhi
Ahle-Chin, Cheen Mein Iran mein sasaani bhi

Isee maamure mein aabaad the yunani bhi
Isee duniya mein yahudi bhi the nasraani bhi

Per tire naam pe talwar uthai kisne
Baat jo bigri hui thi, woh banai kisne

---

1. साकार का पुजारी

Before our arrival, the world presented a strange sight
At places stones were worshipped, at places it was a tree

Humans were used to seeing tangible divinity
And would not believe in God, they couldn't see

Was there anybody there who cared for you?
It was only the strength of Muslims' arms that could your job do

Saljooqs lived here, here lived Turanians
The Chinese in China and Sasanians in Iran

In the world lived Greeks
And the Christian and Jew

But who was it, who rose in arms for your sake to fight
And all that had gone wrong, set right

→

थे हमीं एक तिरे मारका-आराओं में
खुश्कियों में कभी लड़ते, कभी दरियाओं में

दीं अज़ानें कभी योरप के कलीसाओं में
कभी अफ्रीक़ा के तपते हुए सहराओं में

शान आंखों में न जचती थी जहांदारों की
कलमा पढ़ते थे हम छांव में तलवारों की

टल न सकते थे अगर जंग में अड़ जाते थे
पाँव शेरों के भी मैदां से उखड़ जाते थे

तुझ से सरकश हुआ कोई तो बिगड़ जाते थे
तेग क्या चीज़ है हम तोप से लड़ जाते थे

नक़्श तो हीद का हर दिल पे बिठाया हमने
ज़ेरे-ख़ंजर भी यह पैगाम सुनाया हमने

→

The humin ek tire maarka-aaraao mein
khushkiyon mein kabhi larte, kabhi dariyaon mein

din azanen kabhi yorup ke kalisaon mein
kabhi africa ke tapte hue sehraon mein

Shaan aankhon mein na jachti thi jahandaaron ki
kalma parte the hum chhaon mein talvaron ki

Tal na sakte the agar jang mein ar jaate the
paaon sheron ke bhi maidaan se ukhar jaate the

tujh se sarkash hua koi to bigar jaate the
tegh kya cheez hai hum top se lar jaate the

Naqsh toheed ka her dil pe bithaya humne
Zerey-khanzar bhi yeh paigham sunaya humne

We alone your fighter were
We fought on high seas, we fought on land

Sometimes we gave call for prayer in the churches
of Europe
Sometimes, on the red hot African sand

To the vain glory of the lords of the world
We couldn't reconcile

So reciting Kalma under the shadows of the sword
Did we file

Even when the lions would leave and flee,
Once we took the field we retreated not,

We would tolerate not anybody uttering a word
against you

Even when the swords hung over our heads, your
message we delivered
And why only swords, we confronted the cannons too
→

आ गया ऐन लड़ाई में अगर वक्ते-नमाज़
क़िब्लारू होके ज़मीं-बोस हुई क़ौमे-हिजाज़
एक ही सफ़ में खड़े हो गये महमूदो-अयाज़
न कोई बंदा रहा और न कोई बंदानवाज़

बंदा-व-साहबो-मोहताजो-ग़नी एक हुए
तेरी सरकार में पहुँचे तो सभी एक हुए
सफ़ह-ए-दहर[1] से बातिल को मिटाया हमने
नौए-इंसां को ग़ुलामी से छुड़ाया हमने

तेरे काबे को जबीनों से बसाया हमने
तेरे क़ुरआन को सीनों से लगाया हमने
फ़िर भी हमसे यह गिला है कि वफ़ादार नहीं
हम वफ़ादार नहीं तू भी तो दिलदार नहीं!

→

Aa gaya aen larai mein agar waqte-namaz
qiblaru hoke zameen-bose hui qaume-hijaaz
ek hi saf mein khare ho gaye mehmudo-ayaaz
koi banda raha aur na koi bandanawaz
Banda-ve-saahbo-mohtaajo-ghani ek hue
teri sarkar mein pauhnche to sabhi ek hue

Safah-e-dehar se baatil ko mitaya humne
naue-insaan ko ghulami se chhuraya humne

tere kaabe ko jabinon se basaya humne
tere quran ko sino se lagaya humne
Phir bhi humse yeh gila hai ki wafadaar nahin
hum wafadaar nahin tu bhi to dildaar nahin!

---

1. दुनिया

In the heat of the battle if the time for prayer came
The community of Hijaz turned towards Kaaba and
kissed the ground,
In the same row stood Mahmood and Ayyaz
And difference between rich and poor, and master
and slave, no place found

We removed falsehood from the face of the earth
And from slavery, we saved mankind

We filled your Kaaba with rubbing foreheads
And suffused with the Quran, our heart and mind
Even then we're accused of unfaithfulness
If it is so, you too are not kind and generous

→

उम्मतें और भी हैं, उनमें गुनहगार भी हैं
इज्ज़ वाले भी हैं, मस्ते-मये-पिंदार भी हैं

उनमें काहिल भी हैं, ग़ाफ़िल भी हैं, हुशियार भी हैं
सैकड़ों हैं कि तिरे नाम से बेज़ार भी हैं

रहमतें हैं तिरी अग़यार के काशानों पर
बर्क़ गिरती है तो बेचारे मुसलमानों पर

ये शिकायत नहीं, हैं उनके ख़ज़ाने मामूर
नहीं महफिल में जिन्हें बात भी करने का शऊर

क़हर तो यह कि काफ़िर को मिलें हूरो-क़सूर
और बेचारे मुसलमां को फक़त वादा-ए-हूर

अब वह अलताफ़ नहीं हम पे इनायात नहीं
बात ये क्या है कि पहली सी मदारात नहीं

→

Ummatein aur bhi hain, unmein gunehgaar bhi hain
ijz wale bhi hain, maste-maye-pindaar bhi hain

unmein kaahil bhi hain ghaafil bhi hain, hushiar bhi hain
sainkaron hain ki tirey naam se bazaar bhi hain

Rehmatein hain tiri aghyaar ke kaashaano per
Barq girti hai to bechare musalmanon per

Yeh shikayat nahin, hain unke khazane mamoor
nahin mehfil mein jinhen baat bhi karne ka shaour

qahar to yeh ki kafir ko milen huro-qasoor
aur bechare muslaman ko faqat wada-e-hoor

Ab weh altaaf nahin hum pe inayaat nahin
baat yeh kya hai ki pehli si madaraat nahin

There are other communities and they have their sinners too
There are humble people among them as also the vainglorious

Among them are lazy and negligent along with the smart ones
And there are hundreds who don't mind turning their back on you

Still the palaces of others are by your mercy lit
And poor Muslims alone are by the lightening hit!

It is not a complaint though,
Their coffers are full the people who know not even the elementary etiquettes

And the cruel cut is that other get palaces and hoors
While the Muslims get only empty promise of those hoors.

Now your generosity and mercy, we find no more
And find not welcome that we did of yore

→

तेरी महफ़िल भी गई, चाहने वाले भी गये
शब की आहें भी गईं सुबह के नाले भी गये

दिल तुझे दे भी गये अपना सिला ले भी गये
आके बैठे भी न थे और निकाले भी गये

आये उश्शाक़[1], गये वादा-ए-फ़र्दा[2] लेकर
अब उन्हें ढूंढ चिराग़े-रुख़े-ज़ेबा लेकर

Teri mehfil bhi gayee, chahne wale bhi gaye
shab ki aahen bhi gayee subah ke naale bhi gaye

dil tujhe de bhi gaye apna sila le bhi gaye
aake baithe bhi na the aur nikaale bhi gaye

Aaye ushshaaq, gaye wada-e-farda lekar
ab unhen dhoondh chiraghe-rukhe-zeba lekar

---

1. आशिक़ का बहुवचन 2. कल का 'वादा'

The assembly of your faithfuls is no more there
No more are your lovers seen anywhere

Nobody sobs for you at night now, nor in the morning cries
We gave you our sincere devotion, and this is the prize

That we are turned away as soon as we arrive!
Thus came your lover, and with a mere promise of

tomorrow, were turned out of sight
Now look for them with a candle in your hand lit up bright!

जवाबे-शिकवा से

दिल से जो बात निकलती है असर रखती है
पर नहीं, ताक़ते-परवाज़ मगर रखती है
कुदसीउलअस्ल[1] *है रिफ़अत पे नज़र रखती है*
ख़ाक से उठती है गर्दूं पे गुज़र रखती है
इश्क़ था फ़ितनागरी-सरकशो-चालाक मिरा
आस्मां चीर गया नाला-ए-बेबाक मिरा
आई आवाज़ ग़म-अंगेज़ है अफसाना तिरा
अश्के-बेताब से लबरेज़ है पैमाना तिरा
आस्माँगीर हुआ नाला-ए-मस्ताना तिरा
किस तरह शोख़-ज़बाँ है दिले-दीवाना तिरा
शुक्र शिकवे को किया हुस्ने-अदा से तूने
हम-सुख़न कर दिया बन्दे को ख़ुदा से तूने
हम तो मायल-बकरम हैं कोई साइल ही नहीं
राह दिखलायें किसे रहरवे-मंज़िल ही नहीं

→

Dil se jo baat nikalti hai asar rakhati hai
per nahin, taqate-parvaaz magar rakhti hai
kudsiulasal hai rifáet pe nazar rakhati hai
khaaq se uthti hai gardu pe nazar rakhati hai
Ishq tha fitnagari-sarkasho-chalaak mira
aasmaan cheer gaya naala-e-bebaak mira
Aai awaaz gham-angez hai afsana tira
ashke-betaab se labrez hai paimana tira
aasmaangeer hua naala-e-mastana tira
kis tarah shokh-zabaan hai dile-diwana tira
Shukra shikave ko kiya husne-adaa se tune
Humsukhan kar diya bande ko khuda se tune
Hum to maayal-bakram hain koi saaiel hi nahin
raah dikhlayen kise reharve-manzil hi nahin

---

1. फरिश्तों के कुल से

Excerpts from Reply to the Complaint

It is never in vain, if it is a sincere cry
It may not have wings, but it is bound to fly

Belong as it does to the family of the birds
It rises from the earth and reaches the sky

My cry was a cry of love, a cry of rebellion
It pierced the sky and soon reached the heaven

And a voice came: your tale is sad indeed
Your heart is indeed welling up with grief

Your cry has spread around every where
Your heart is indeed a wonderful lair

Good, that you have made your complaint with grace
And brought man before God face of face

I am willing to oblige, but nobody deserves my favour
Who should I guide when there is no seeker

→

तरबियत[1] आम तो है, जौहरे-क़ाबिल ही नहीं
जिस से तामीर हो आदम की यह वह गिल ही नहीं
जिन को आता नहीं दुनिया में कोई फ़न तुम हो
नहीं जिस क़ौम को परवा-ए-नशेमन तुम हो
बिजलियां जिस में हों पोशीदा वह खिरमन तुम हो
बेच खाते हैं जो अस्लाफ़[2] के मदफ़न तुम हो
हो निको-नाम जो कब्रों की तिजारत करके
क्या न बेचोगे जो मिल जायें सनम पत्थर के

मुनफ़अत[3] एक है इस क़ौम की नुक़सान भी एक
एक ही सब का नबी, दीन भी, ईमान भी एक
हरमे-पाक भी, अल्लाह भी, कुर्आन भी एक
कुछ बड़ी बात थी होते जो मुसलमान भी एक
फ़िरक़ा-बन्दी है कहीं और कहीं ज़ाते हैं
क्या ज़माने में पनपने की यही बातें हैं

tarbiyat aam to hai, jauhare-qabil hi nahin
jis se taamir ho aadam ki yeh woh gil hi nahin

Jinko aata nahin duniyan mein koi fun tum ho
nahin jis qaum ko parva-e-nasheman tum ho
bijliyan jis mein hon paushida woh khirman tum ho
bech khaate hain jo aslaaf ke madfan tum ho
Ho niko-naam jo qabron ki tijarat karke
kya na bechoge jo mil jayen sanam pather ke

Munfáet ek hai is qaum ki nuksaan bhi ek
ek hi sab ka nabee, deen bhi, imaan bhi ek
harme-paak bhi, allah bhi, quraan bhi ek
kuchh bari baat thi hote jo musalmaan bhi ek
Firqa bandi hai kahin aur kahin zaatein hain
kya zamane mein panapne ki yahi baatein hain

---

1. प्रशिक्षण 2. पूर्वज 3. लाभ

I see no one who doth business mean
The clay that makes man is not to be seen
Your are the ones who lack all skill
You are the ones who for their abode care not
You are the granary fit for the lightening to hit
The ones who can their forefathers' burial ground sell
You are the ones known for trading in graves
The ones who will barter away anything for the stone-gods' sake

The gain and loss of a community is common to all its members
They have one God, one faith, one Kaaba, one Quran
If only the Muslims were one, they wouldn't have into misery gone
But they are divided in castes, in various sects dispersed
Is this the way for communities to flourish in the world?

ख़ुशामद

मैं कारे-जहां से नहीं आगाह व लेकिन
अरबाबे-नज़र से नहीं पोशीदा कोई राज़

कर तू भी हकूमत के वज़ीरों की ख़ुशामद
दस्तूर नया और नये दौर का आग़ाज़

मालूम नहीं है ये ख़ुशामद की हक़ीक़त
कह दे कोई उल्लू को अगर रात का शहबाज़

Main kaare-jahan se nahin aagaah lekin
arbaabe-nazar se nahin poshida koi raaz

Kar tu kabhi hukumat ke waziron ki khushamad
dastoor naya aur naye daur ka aaghaaz

Maloom nahin hai ye khushamad ki haqiqat
keh de koi ulloo ko agar raat ka shehbaaz

Flattery

I am not well versed in the affairs of the world though,

Nothing is hidden from a seeing eye
In this new disposition and in the new era, I know

You too should flatter the powers that be
Calling an owl a nocturnal eagle—
Herein lies the beauty of flattery

गिला

मालूम किसे हिंद की तक़दीर कि अब तक
बेचारा किसी ताज का ताबिंदा नगीं है

दहक़ां है किसी कब्र का उगला हुआ मुर्दा
बोसीदा कफ़न जिसका अभी ज़ेरे-ज़मीं है

जां भी गरवे-ग़ैर, बदन भी गरवे-ग़ैर
अफ़सोस की बाक़ी न मकां है न मकीं है

योरुप की ग़ुलामी पे रज़ामंद हुआ तू
मुझको तो गिला तुझसे है योरुप से नहीं है

Maloom kise hind ki taqdeer ki ab tak
bechara kisi taaj ka tabinda nagin hai

Dehkan hai kisi qabr ka ugla hua murda
boseeda kafan jiska abhi zerey-zamin hai

Jaan bhi garve-ghair, badan bhi garve-ghair
afsos ki baaqi na makaan hai na makin hai

Yorup ki ghulami pe razamand hua tu
mujhko to gila tujhse hai yorup se nahin hai

A Chastisement

Who can describe your sad plight, my India
You are a jewel only for somebody else's crown

Your present is like a carcass belched out by the grave
While the coffin still lies buried under gound,

Your body and soul, alas are mortgage to alien rule!
It is because of your own weakness that the European
roughshod ride

I blame not Europe therefore, it is you I would chide.

दाग़[1]

अज़्मते-ग़ालिब है इक मुद्दत से पैवंदे-ज़मीं
मेहदी-ए-मजरूह है शहरे-ख़ामोशां का मकीं
तोड़ डाली मौत ने गुर्बत में मीना-ए-अमीर
चश्मे-महफ़िल में है अब तक कैफ़े-सहबाए-अमीर
आज लेकिन हमनवा! सारा चमन मातम में है
शम-ए-रोशन बुझ गई, बज़्मे-सुख़न मातम में है
बुलबुले-दिल्ली ने बांधा उस चमन में आशियां
हमनवा हैं सब अनादिल, बाग़े-हस्ती के जहाँ
चल बसा दाग़, आह मैय्यत उसकी ज़ेबे-दोश[2] है
आख़िरी शायर जहानाबाद का खामोश है।
अब कहां वह बांकपन, वह शोखी-ए-तर्ज़े-बयां
आग थी काफ़ूरे-पीरी में जवानी की निहां

→

Azmate-ghalib hai ik muddat se paivand-zameen
mehdi-e-Majrooh hai shehre-khamoshaan ka makeen
Tor daali maut ne ghurbat mein meena-e-ameer
chashme-mehfil mein hai ab tak kaife-sehbaae-Ameer
Aaj lekin humnava ! saara chaman maatam mein hai
sham-e-roshan bujh gayee, bazme-sukhan maatam mein hai
Bulbule-dilli ne bandha us chaman mein aashyaan
humnava hain sab anadil, baghe-hasti ke jahaan
Chal basa Daagh, aah maiyat uski zebey-dosh hai
aakhiri shayar jahanabaad ka khamosh hai
Ab kahan woh baankpan, woh shokhi-e-tarze-bayaan
aag thi kaafure-peeri mein jawani ki nihaan

---

1. उर्दू के मशहूर शायर और इक़बाल के उस्ताद 'दाग़' देहलवी 2. कब्र की शोभा

Daagh

Great Ghalib has long been buried now
Mehdi Majrooh is a denizen of the land of the dead already
The wine-jug of Amear was broken by death when he was still in exile
Though that wine intoxicates the mehfil still,
But today my friend, the whole garden is mourning,
In mourning is the world of poetry, for its bright light is gone—
The nightingale of Delhi resided in this garden.
Daagh has departed and on our shoulders we carry his honoured corpse,
The last poet of Jahanabad has fallen silent today.
Where shall we find that rakishness, that brightness of expression now
Even in old age, he radiated the glow of youth.

→

Daagh (1831-1905) : A front rank Urdu poet, known for exquisite romantic poetry and for writing in simple conversational Urdu.

थी ज़ुबाने-दाग़ पर जो आरज़ू हर दिल में है
लैला-ए-मानी वहां बेपर्दा, यां महमिल में है
अब सबा से कौन पूछेगा सकूते-गुल[1] का राज़
कौन समझेगा चमन में नाला-ए-बुलबुल का राज़
थी हक़ीकत से न ग़फलत फ़िक्र की परवाज़ में
आंख तायर की नशेमन पर रही परवाज़ में
और दिखलायेंगे मज़्मूं की हमें बारीकियां
अपने फ़िक्रे-नुक्ता-आरा[2] की फ़लक-पैमाइयां[3]
तल्ख़ी-ए-दौरां के नक़्शे खेंच कर रुलवायेंगे
या तख़य्युल की नई दुनिया हमें दिखलायेंगे
इस चमन में होंगे पैदा बुलबुले-शीराज़ भी
सैकड़ों साहिर भी होंगे, साहिबे-एजाज़[4] भी

→

Thi Zubane-Daagh per jo aarzoo her dil mein hai
laila-e-maani wahan beparda, yaan mehmill mein hai
Ab saba se kaun puchhega sakute-gul ka raaz
kaun samjhega chaman mein naaala-e-bulbul ka raaz
Thi haqiqat se na ghaflat fikra ki parvaaz mein
aankh taayer ki nasheman per rahi parvaaz mein
Aur dikhlyenge mamun ki humein bareekiyan
apne phikre-nukta-aara ki phalak-paimaaiyaan
Talkhi-e-dauraan ke naqshc khench kar rulvayenge
ya takhaiyul ki nai duniya humein dikhlayenge
Is chaman mein honge paida bulbule-shiraaz bhi
sainkaron saahir bhi honge, sahibe-aejaz bhi

---

1. फूल की खामोशी 2. सूक्ष्म चिंतन 3. आकाश नापना 4. चमत्कार दिखाने वाले

Everybody wants to emulate his style.
In his case, the laila of meaning sits on the litter unveiled.
Who will ask the morning breeze now why the rose is silent!
Who will tell us now what the wail of the nightingale in the garden means!
Like the eye of the bird fixed on his nest during the flight
He never lost touch with the earth even when his fancy flew;
Others will show us the subtleties of their subject
They will reveal their thought soaring sky high,
Make us cry by portraying the cruelty of the age
Or show the world of their imagination's making,
There'll be many magician, many who can cast a spell,
The nightingale of Shiraz too will be born here

→

उट्ठेंगे आज़र हज़ारों शेर के बुतख़ाने से
मय पिलायेंगे नए साक़ी नए पैमाने से
लिक्खी जायेंगी किताबे-दिल की तफ्सीरें बहुत
होंगी ऐ ख्वाबे-जवानी तेरी ताबीरें बहुत
हूबहू खींचेगा लेकिन इश्क़ की तस्वीर कौन
उठ गया नावक-फ़गन, मारेगा दिल पर तीर कौन
अश्क के दाने ज़मीने-शेर में बोता हूं मैं
तू भी रो ऐ ख़ाके-दिल्ली दाग़ को रोता हूं मैं
ऐ जहानाबाद! ऐ सरमाया-ए-बज़्मे-सुख़न
हो गया फिर आज पामाले-ख़ज़ाँ तेरा चमन
वो गुले-रंगीं तिरा रुख़सत मिसाले-बू हुआ
आह! ख़ाली दाग़ से, काशना-ए उर्दू हुआ
थी न शायद कुछ कशिश ऐसी वतन की ख़ाक़ में
वह महे-कामिल हुआ पिन्हां दकन की ख़ाक में

→

Utthenge aazar hazaron sher ke butkhane se
mai pilayenge naye saaqi naye paimane se
Likhi jaayengi kitabe-dil ki tafseerein bahut
hongi ae khawabe-jawani teri taabirein bahut
Hubahu khinchega lekin ishq ki tasveer kaun
uth gaya navak-fagan, maarega dil per teer kaun
Ashk ke daane zamine-sher mein bota hun main
tu bhi ro ae khaaqe-Dilli Daagh ko rota hun main
Ae jahanabaad ! ae sarmaya-e-bazme-sukhan
ho gaya phir aaj paamale-khazaan tera chaman
Woh gule-rangin tira rukhsat misaale-bu hua
aah ! khali Daagh se, kaashaana-e-Urdu hua
thi na shayad kuchh kashis aisi vatan ki khaaq mein
woh mahe-kaamil hua pinhaan dakan ki khaaq mein

But who will draw the precise picture of love,
Who will hit the heart straight?

I sow my tears in the field of verse
O Jahanabad, O hub of poetry, let you also cry
For your garden lies wasted by autumn once more
Its fragrance has left it high and dry.
Alas, the house of Urdu has lost Daagh!
The land of his birth had lost attraction, perhaps
So the full moon moved away and set in the Deccan.
Those who were worthy of being saqi, are gone
And the tavern wears a deserted look
Only in Hali now, some glory of Delhi remains.

Cruel death makes us weep tears of blood
For the hunter has shot his arrow in the dark;

→

उठ गए साक़ी जो थे मयख़ाना ख़ाली रह गया
यादगारे बज़्में देहली एक हाली रह गया
आरज़ू को खून रुलवाती है बेदादे-अजल
मारता है तीर तारीकी में सय्यादे-अजल
खुल नहीं सकती शिकायत के लिए लेकिन ज़ुबाँ
है ख़ज़ाँ का रंग भी वजहे-क़यामे-गुलिस्तां
एक ही क़ानूने-आलमगीर के हैं सब असर
बूए-गुल का बाग़ से, गुलचीं का दुनिया से सफ़र

Uth gaye saqi jo the, Me-Khana Khalireh gaya
yaad gaare bazm Delhi ek Hali reh gaya
Aarzoo ko khoon rulwati hai bedaade-ajal
maarta hai teer tareeki mein saiyade-ajal
Khul nahin sakti shikayat ke liye lekin zubaan
hai khizaan ka rang bhi wajahe-qayame-gulistan
Ek hi qanoone-aalamgeer ke hain sab asar
bue-gul ka baagh se gulchin ka duniya se safar

But knowing that autumn too is part of the garden's life,
We complain not
For the law of departure of fragrance from the garden,
and the grandeur from the world governs the entire world.
Thousands of Aazars will arise from the temple of the Muse
New Saqis will serve us wine in new cups
Many a commentary will be written on the book of the heart
The dream of youth will be interpreted in a hundred ways,

इंसान

क़ुदरत का अजीब यह सितम है!
इंसान को राज़जू[1] बनाया
राज़ उस की निगाह से छिपाया
बेताब है ज़ोक़-आगही[2] का
खुलता नहीं भेद ज़िंदगी का
हैरते आग़ाज़ो-इंतहा है
आईने के घर में और क्या है
है गर्मे-ख़राम मौजे-दरिया
दरिया सू-ए-बहर[3] जादा-पैमा[4]
बादल को हवा उड़ा रही है
शानो पे उठाये ला रही है
तारे, मस्ते-शराबे-तक़दीर
ज़िंदाने-फलक में पा बज़ंजीर

Qudrat ka ajeeb yeh sitam hai →
insaan ko raazju banaya
Raaz us ki nigaah se chhipaya
betaab hai zoq-aagahi ka
khulta nahin bhed zindagi ka
Hairate aaghaazo-intaha hai
aaine ke ghar mein aur kya hai
Hai garme-kharaam mauje-dariya
dariya su-e-behar jaada-paima
Baadal ko hawa ura rahi hai
shano pe uthaye la rahi hai
Taare, maste-sharabe-taqdeer
Zindane-phalak mein paa-b-ba-zanjeer

---

1. रहस्य खोजने वाला 2. ज्ञान 3. समुद्र की ओर 4. चलने वाला यात्री

Man

It's cruel joke of Nature
That man is created a seeker of secrets
And the secrets are kept hidden from his eye;
His desire for knowledge is so intense indeed
But the secret of life, unto him opens not.

His end is a mystery, mystery the beginning
His life is a house of mirrors end to end;

The wave of the river is gliding along
And the river is heading towards the sea;
Carrying them upon its shoulders
The wind is sweeping the clouds clean;
Themselves imprisoned and chained in the sky
The stars strut about drunk as arbiters of destiny,

→

ख़ुर्शीद वह आबिदे-सहर-खेज़
लाने वाला पयामे-"बरखेज़"

मग़रिब की पहाड़ियों में छिपकर
पीता है मये-शफ़क़ का साग़र

लज़्ज़तगीरे-वजूद हर शय
सरमस्ते-मये-नमूद हर शय

कोई नहीं ग़मगुसारे-इंसां
क्या तल्ख़ है रोज़गारे-इंसां

Khurshid, woh aabide-sehar-khez
laane wala payame-'barkhez'

Məghrib ki pahariyon mein chhipkar
peeta hai maye-shafaq ka saaghar

Lazzatgeere-wajood her shay
sarmaste-maye-namood her shay

Koi nahin ghamgusare-insaan
kya talkh hai rozgaare-insaan

Getting up early, the worshipper of dawn,
The sun heralds the arrival of the morn

Then hiding behind the western hill
Drinks red wine to its fill.

Every object is drunk with its being
Every object is enjoying its existence

Nobody cares at all for man
What a cruel call for man!

आज और कल

वो कल-के ग़मो-ऐश पे कुछ हक नहीं रखता
जो आज ख़ुद अफ़रोज़ो-जिगर-सोज़ नहीं है

वो क़ौम नहीं लायिक़े-हंगामा-ए-फ़रदा
जिस क़ौम की तक़दीर में इमरोज़ नहीं है

Woh kal ke ghamo-aish pe haq nahin rakhata
jo aaj khud afrozo-jigar-soz nahin hai

Woh qaum nahin laayiqe-hungama-e-farda
jis qaum ki taqdeer mein imroz nahin hai

Today and Tomorrow

He deserves not the joys and sorrows of tomorrow
Whose heart beats not with the current of today

A nation, not coming to grips with its tumultuous present
Can hardly to the triumphs of tomorrow a claim lay

क़ौम ने पैग़ामे-गौतम की ज़रा परवा न की
क़द्र पहचानी न अपने गोहरे-यकदाना की

आह! बदक़िस्मत रहे आवाज़े-हक़ से बेख़बर
ग़ाफ़िल अपने फल की शीरीनी से होता है शजर

आशकार उसने किया जो ज़िंदगी का राज़ था
हिंद को लेकिन ख़्याली फ़लसफ़े पर नाज़ था

शमए-हक़ से जो मुनव्वर हो यह वह महफ़िल न थी
बारिशे-रहमत हुई लेकिन ज़मीं क़ाबिल न थी।

→

Qaum ne paghame-gautam ki zara parva na ki
qadr pehchani na apne gohare-yakdana ki

Aah ! badqismat rahe awaaze-huq se bekhabar
ghafil apne phal ki shereeni se hota hai shajar

Aashkaar usne kiya jo zindgi ka raaz tha
hind ko lekin khayali falsaph per naaz tha

Shammáe huq se jo munavvar ho ye woh mehfil na thi
barishe-rehmat hui lekin zameen qabil na thi

Nanak

This country did not value the message of
Gautam Buddha
It did not recognize the true worth of its
matchless pearl,

Like the tree that knows not the sweetness of
its own fruit

The unfortunate nation heard not the voice of truth;
Gautam Buddha revealed to us the meaning of life

But India was fixated on fanciful philosophies
This was not a land willing to be lit by the
lamp of truth

The rain of mercy came but the land was
not ready for it,

→

आह! शूदर के लिए हिंदोस्तां ग़म खाना है
दर्दे-इंसानी से इस बस्ती का दिल बेगाना है

बरहमन सरशार है अब तक मये-पिंदार में
शमए-गौतम जल रही है महफ़िले अग़यार में

बुतकदा फिर बाद मुद्दत के मगर रोशन हुआ
नूरे-इब्राहीम से आज़र का घर रोशन हुआ

फिर उठी आख़िर सदा तौहीद की पंजाब से
हिंद को इक मर्दे-कामिल ने जगाया ख़्वाब से

Aah ! shudar ke liye hindostan ghuam khana hai
darde-insaani se is basti ka dil begana hai

Brahman sarshaar hai ab tak maye-pindaar mein
shammáe-gautam jal rahi hai mehfile-aghyaar mein

Butkada phir baad muddat ke magar roshan hua
noore-ibrahim se aazar ka ghar roshan hua

Phir uthi aakhir sada tauheed ki punjab se
hind ko ik marde-kaamil ne jagaya khawab se

It knows not the thing called human sympathy,
For the shudras in particular it is land of misery

While the light that Gautam lit, shines abroad
The Brahman is here, in his own pride bound,

Much like Azar house that was by Abraham lit
This land at last saw the light,

Once again the message of God's oneness
came from Panjab

And India was woken up from slumber by a perfect
man of spiritual might

शमा और शायर

मुझको जो मौजे-नफ़स देती है पैग़ामे-अजल[1]
लब उसी मौजे-नफ़स से है नवां-पैरा तेरा

मैं तो जलती हूं कि है मुज़मिर[2] मेरी फ़ितरत में सोज़
तू फ़रोज़ां है कि परवानों को हो सौदा तेरा

यूं तो रोशन है; मगर सोज़े-दरूं रखता नहीं
शो'ला है मिस्ले-चिराग़े-लाला-ए-सहरा तेरा

सोच तू दिल में लक़ब[3] साक़ी का है ज़ेबा तुझे
अंजुमन प्यासी है और पैमाना बे-सहबा[4] तेरा

क़ैस पैदा हों तेरी महफ़िल में! यह मुमकिन नहीं
तंग है सहरा तेरा, महमिल है बे-लैला तेरा

था जिन्हें ज़ौक़े-तमाशा, वो तो रुख़सत हो गए
लेके अब तू वादा-ए-दीदारे-आम आया तो क्या

→

Mujhko jo mauje-nafas deti hai paighame-ajal
lab usee mauje-nafas se hai nava-paira tera

Main to jalti hoon ki hai muzmir meri fitrat mein soz
tu farozan hai ki parvanon ko ho sauda tera

Yun to roshan hai; magar soze-darun rakhata nahin
shola hai misle-chirage-laala-e-sehra tera

Soch tu dil mein laqab saaqi ka hai zeba tujhe
anjuman pyasi hai aur paimana be-sehba tera

Qais paida hon teri mehfil mein yeh mumkin nahin
tang hai sehra tera, mehmil hai be-laila tera

Tha jinhen zauqe-tamasha, woh to rukhsat ho gaye
leke ab tu wada-e-deedare-aam aaya to kya

---

1. मौत का संदेश 2. निहित 3. उपनाम 4. शराब से खाली

The Candle and the Poet

The breath that heralds my death,
The same breath enables you to sing,

I burn because it is my nature
You glow because you want to show off,

So that you are emulated by the moth;
You may be shining but you are bereft of inner fire—
A spark you are, but no better than the rose of the desert;

When the whole mehfil is thirsty and your own cup is empty
Do you think the pseudonym 'Saqi' behoves you?

Narrow is you dessert, and without Laila on its back, your camel
Your mehfil never can a Qais produce.

Those who were yearning for your sight are no longer around
What if you hold now a promise of public view!

→

अंजुमन से वो पुराने शोला-आशाम[1] उठ गए
साक़िया! महफ़िल में तू आतिश-ब-जाम आया तो क्या

आख़िरे-शब दीद के क़ाबिल थी बिस्मिल की तड़प
सुबह-दम कोई अगर बाला-ए-बाम आया तो क्या

शम्मअ-महफ़िल होके तू जब सोज़ से ख़ाली रहा
तेरे परवाने भी इस लज़्ज़त से बेगाना रहे

रिश्ता-ए-उल्फ़त में जब इनको पिरो सकता था तू
फिर परेशां क्यों तेरी तसबीह के दाने रहे

शौक़े-बेपरवा गया, फ़िक्रे-फ़लक-पैमा गया।
तेरी महफ़िल में न दीवाने न फ़रज़ाने रहे॥

ख़ैर, तू साक़ी सही, लेकिन पिलाएगा किसे?
अब तो वो मैकश रहे बाक़ी न मैख़ाने रहे

→

Anjuman se woh purane shola-aashaam uth gaye
saaqiya ! mehfil mein tu aatish-ba-jaam aaya to kya

Aakhire-shab deed ke qabil thi bismil ki tarap
subah-dam koi agar baala-e-baam aaya to kya

Shammáe-mehfil hoke tu jab soz se khali raha
tere parvane bhi is lazzat se begana rahe

Rishta-e-ulfat mein jab inko piro sakta tha tu
phir pareshan kyon teri tasbeeh ke daane rahe

Shauqe-beperwa gaya, fiqre-falak-paima gaya
teri mehfil mein na deewane na farzane rahe

Khair, tu saaqi sahi, lekin pilayega kise
Jab to woh maikash rahe baaqi na maikhane rahe

---

1. आग पीने वाला शराबी

The mehfil is already empty of those who drank red hot wine
What if you offer now cups of fiery stuff, O Saqi !

As the night was ending, the condition of the wounded one was indeed a sight to see
What if somebody comes to the terrace now after the dawn has descended!

You yourself are bereft of fire even though you are the mehfil's candle
Is it any wonder then the moths around you experience not the delight, they should?

Why do they lie scattered, the beads of your garleand
Even though through love you could knit them together?

Your care-free attitude is gone, gone is your sky-scaling flight
In your mehfil now are seen neither the burning moths nor the men of wisdom.

You may be Saqi still, but whom will you give the drink
For, now there are neither those drinkers nor the taverns around,

→

रो रही है आज इक टूटी हुई मीना उसे
कल तलक गर्दिश में जिस साक़ी के पैमाने रहे

आज हैं खामोश वो दश्ते-जुनूं-परवर जहां
रक़्स में लैला रही, लैला के दीवाने रहे

वाए नाकामी मता-ए-कारवां जाता रहा
कारवां के दिल से अहसासे-ज़ियां जाता रहा

जिनके हंगामों से थे आबाद वीराने कभी
शहर उनके मिट गए आबादियां बन हो गईं

तू अगर खुद्दार है मिन्नतकशे-साक़ी न हो
ऐन दरिया में हबाब-आसा-नंगू[2] पैमाना कर

कैफ़ियत बाक़ी पुराने कोहो-सहरा में नहीं
है जूनूं तेरा नया, पैदा नया वीराना कर

→

Ro rahi hai aaj ik tooti hui meena use
kal talak gardish mein jis saaqi ke paimane rahe

Aaj hain khamosh woh dashte-junoon-parvar jahan
raqs mein laila rahi, laila ke deewane rahe

Waae nakamai mata-e-kaarwan jaata raha
kaarwan ke dil se ahsaase-ziyan jaata raha

Jinke hungamon se the aabaad veerane kabhi
shehar unke mit gaye, aabadiyan van ho gayeen

Tu agar khuddar hai minnatkashe-saaqi na ho
aen dariya mein habaab-aasa-nagun paimana kar

Kaifiyat baaqi purane koho-sehra mein nahin
hai junoon tera naya, paida naya veerana kar

---

1. लुटने का अहसास 2. पानी के बुलबुले की तरह टेढ़ा

Now the very wine-pot mourns the loss of the Saqi
Because of whom till yesterday only the
taverns flourished;

The fertile field where fiery passion grew, lies
barren now
Neither Laila nor her lovers in frenzy are now seen,

How sad that the caravan has been robbed of
its belongings
And those in the caravan feel not the loss!

Those, because of whom the wilderness was
once bustling
Even their cities have turned wastelands now,

If you are self-respecting, do not cringe before
the Saqi,
From the very source of wine fill your cup,

The mountain and the desert of the old will not
serve your purpose great
Your passion is unique, so a new wilderness create,

→

आशना अपनी हक़ीक़त से हो ऐ दहक़ां[1] जरा
दाना तू, खेती भी तू, बारां भी तू, हासिल भी तू

आह जिसकी जुस्तजू आवारा रखती है तुझे
राह तू, रहरौ[2] भी तू, रहबर भी तू, मंज़िल भी तू

कांपता है दिल तेरा, अंदेशा-ए-तूफ़ां से क्या
नाखुदा तू, बह्र तू, कश्ती भी तू, साहिल भी तू

देख आकर कूचा-ए-चाके-गिरेबा में कभी
क़ैस तू, लैला भी तू, सहरा भी तू, महमिल भी तू

वाए नादानी! कि तू मोहताजे-साक़ी हो गया
मय भी तू, मीना भी तू, साक़ी भी तू, महफ़िल भी तू

बेख़बर! तू जौहरे-आईना-ए-अय्याम[3] है
तू ज़माने में खुदा का आखिरी पैग़ाम है

Aashana apni haqiqat se ho ae dehqan zara
dana tu, kheti bhi tu, baaraan bhi tu, hasil bhi tu

aah jiski justju awara rakhati hai tujhe
raah tu, rehrau bhi tu, rehbar bhi tu, manzil bhi tu

Kaanpta hai dil tera, andesha-e-tufaan se kya
nakhuda tu, behr tu, kashti bhi tu, sahil bhi tu

Dekh aakar kucha-e-chaake-gireban mein kabhi
qais tu, laila bhi tu, sehra bhi tu, mehmil bhi tu

Waae nadani ! ki tu mohtaje-saaqi ho gaya
mai bhi tu, meena bhi tu, saaqi bhi tu, mehfil bhi tu

Bekhabar ! tu jauhare-aaina-e-aiyaam hai
tu zamane mein Khuda ka aakhiri paigham hai

---

1. किसान 2. पथिक 3. समय का सार

Know your own worth, O tiller of the land
You are the field, you are the grain, you are the rain,
you are the crop,

What are you searching around, why don't you know
You're the path, you're the traveller, you're the guide
and the destination tool

Why do you tremble for fear of the gale
You're the boatman, you're the boat and you are
the shore,

Come sometime in love's lane and see for yourself
You are the Majnu, you are Laila and you herseat
on the camel-back,

What a pity that you should be dependent on the
Saqi
While you're the wine, you're the pitcher, you're the
Saqi and you're mehfil yourseelf!

The final message of God on earth;
You're the very essence of the age, O ignorant one,
Know your worth.

ये मेहर है बेमहरिये-सय्याद का पर्दा
आई न मेरे काम तेरी ताज़ा सबूरी

रखने लगा मुरझाये हुए फूल क़फ़स में
शायद कि असीरों को गवारा है असीरी

Ye mehar hai bemehariya-saiyaad ka parda
aai na mere kaam teri taaza saburi

Rakhne laga murjhaye hue phool qafas mein
shayad ki aseeron ko ganwara hai aseeri

Psychology of Power

The pity that the hunter shows me is rather cruel
His trick is useless, really,

He is now keeping withered flowers in the cage
Hoping that I would thus adjust to slavery.

खिज़रे-राह

साहिले दरिया पे मैं इक रात था महवे-नज़र
गोशा-ए-दिल में छिपाये इक जहाने-इज़्तराब
शब सकूत-अफ़ज़ा, हवा-आसूदा, दरिया नर्म-सैर,
थी नज़र हैरां कि यह दरिया है या तस्वीरे आब
जैसे गहवारे में सो जाता है तिफ़्ले शीर-ख्वार,
मौजे-मुज़तर थी कहीं गहराइयों में मस्ते-ख्वाब
रात के अफ़सूं से तायर आशियानों में असीर,
अंजुमे-कम-ज़ौ गिरफ्तारे-तलिस्मे माहताब
देखता क्या हूं कि वह पैके-जहां-पैमाँ[1] खिज़र,
जिसकी पीरी में है मानन्दे-सहर रंगे-शबाब
कह रहा है मुझसे ऐ जोया-ए असरारे-अज़ल,
चश्मे दिल वा हो तो है तक़दीरे-आलम बे-हिजाब
दिल में यह सुनकर बरपा हंगामा-ए महशर हुआ,
मैं शहीदे-जुस्तजू था यों सुखन-गुस्तर हुआ

→

Sahile dariya pe main ek raat tha mehave-nazar
gosha-e-dil mein chhipaye ik jahane-iztaraab
Shab sakut-afza, hawa-aasuda, dariya narm-sair
thi nazar hairan ki yeh dariya hai ya tasveere-aab
Jaise gehware mein so jaata hai tifle sheer-khawar
mauje-muztar thi kahin gehraiyon mein maste-khawab
Raat ke aphsun se taayar aashiyanon mein aseer
anjume-kam-jo giraftare-talisme maahtaab
Dekhta kya hun ki woh paike-jahan-paima Khizar
jiski peeri mein hai maanande-sehare range-shabaab
Keh raha hai tujhse ae joya-e asraare-azal
chashme dil waa ho to hai taqdeere-aalam be-hijaab
Dil mein yeh sunkar barpa hungama-e mehshar hua
main shaheede justju tha yon sukhan-gustar hua

---

1. सृष्टि का रहस्य

Khizar–The Guide

With a storm raging in the heart last night
I stood on the bank of the river intently watching

The night was clothed in silence, and the breeze
softly blew
The calm river looked more like a painted sheet
of water
And like a suckling babe in the cradle
Without a ruffle on the surface, fast asleep

Even as the birds in their nests peacefully slept
And the stars dimmed by the moonlight lustreless
stood

Suddenly I see Khizar, who knows the secrets of
the world
And who in old age too looks in youth glows;

Addressing me he says that if the soul is awake
The whole world becomes an open book.

Seeker that I am, I heard this,
It stirred me and I said :

→

ऐ तिरी चश्मे-जहां-बीं पर वह तूफां आशकार,
जिनके हंगामे अभी दरिया में सोते हैं खमोश
छोड़कर आबादियां रहता है तू सहरा-नवर्द,
ज़िंदगी तेरी है बे-रोज़ो-शबो-फरदा-व-दोश
ज़िंदगी का राज़ क्या है, सल्तनत क्या चीज़ है
और यह सरमाया-व-मेहनत में है कैसा ख़रोश [1]
हो रहा है एशिया का खर्क़ा-ए-दैरीना चाक,
नौजवां अक़वामे-नौ, दौलत के हैं पैराया-पोश
गर्चे असकंदर रहा महरूमे-आबे-ज़िंदगी,
फ़ितरते-असकंदरी अब तक है गर्मे-नायो-नोश
बेचता है हाशिमी नामूसे-दीने-मुस्तफा,
खाक़ो-खूं में मिल रहा है, तुर्कमाने-सख्त कोश
आग है, औलादे-इब्राहीम है, नमरूद है,
क्या किसी को फिर किसी का इम्तहां मक़सूद है?

Ae tiri chashme-jahaan-been per woh tufaan aashkaar
jinke hungame abhi dariya mein sote hain khamosh
Kashti-e-miskeeno-jaane paako-deeware-yateem
ilme-Moosa bhi hai tere saamne hairat-farosh
Chhorkar aabadiyan rehta hai tu sehra-navard
zindgi teri hai be-rozo-shabo-pharda-wa-dosh
Zindagi ka raaz kya hai, saltanat kya cheez hai
aur yeh sarmaya-wa-mehnat mein hai kaisa kharosh
Ho raha hai ashiya ka kharqa-e-daireena chaak
naujawan aqwame-nau, daulat ke hain pairaya-posh
Garche askandar raha mehrume-aabe-zindgi
fitratey-askandari ab tak hai garme-nayo-nosh
Bechita hai hashimi naamuse-deene-Mustafa
khako-khoon mein mil raha hai, turkemane-sakht kosh
Aag hai, aulaade-Ibrahim hai, namrud hai
kya kisi ko phir kisi ka imtihaan maqsood hai

You who can see into the future
What is hidden as yet from the ordinary ken

You who prefer wilderness to human habitation
And are free from the cycle of day and night,

Say what is life, what is its secret
What is kingdom, why is there tussle
Between labour and capital?

Asia's grey gown is in tatters
And its youth apes the materialism of the west

Although Sikander couldn't get the elixir of life
The tendency he represents is very much alive;

The descendants of prophet Mohammod are selling
his faith in the marketplace
While the hardy Turkimistanis are being ground
to dust;
We have a huge fire ready, we have the progeny of
Ibrahim as also we have Namrood
Is somebody's trial by fire on the anvil again!

ज़िंदगी

बरतर अज़ अंदेशा-ए-सूदो-ज़ियां है ज़िंदगी
है कभी जां और कभी तस्लीमे-जां है ज़िंदगी
तू इसे पैमाना-ए-इमरोज़ो-फ़रदा से न नाप
जावदां, पैहम रवां, हर दम जवां है ज़िंदगी
अपनी दुनिया आप पैदा कर अगर ज़िंदों में है
सिर्रे-आदम है ज़मीरे-कुल फ़का[1] है ज़िंदगी
ज़िंदगानी की हक़ीक़त कोहकन के दिल से पूछ
जूए-शीरो-तेशा-व-संगे-गरा[2] है ज़िंदगी
बंदगी में घुटके रह जाती है इक जू-ए-कम-आब
और आज़ादी में बहरे-बेकरां है ज़िंदगी
आशकारा है यह अपनी कुव्वते-तसखीर से
गरचे इक मिट्टी के पैकर में निहां है ज़िंदगी
कुलज़मे-हस्ती से तू उभरा है मानन्दे हबाब
इस जयां-खाने में तेरा इम्तहां है ज़िंदगी

→

Bartar az andesha-e-sudo-ziyan hai zindagi
Hai kabhi jaan aur kabhi tasleeme-jaan hai zindagi
Tu ise paimane-e-imrozo-pharda se na naap
Javadan, paiham ravan, hardam-jawan hai zindagi
Apni duniya aap paida kar agar zindon mein hai
Sirre-adam hai zameene-kul phakan hai zindagi
Zindagani ki haquiqat kohkan ke dil se puchh
Jue-sheero-tesha-va-sange-gara hai zindagi
Bandagi mein ghutke rah jati hai ik jue-kam-aab
Aur azadi mein bahre-bekaran hai zindagi
Aashkara hai yeh apni kuvvate taskheer se
Garche ik mitti ke packer mein nihan hai zindagi
Kulzame-hasti se tu ubhara hai manande habab
Is jayan-khane me tera imtahan hai zindagi

---

1. मानव जाति का रहस्य, 2. फरहाद।

Life

Life transcends gain or loss
It sometimes means living, sometimes dying
Measure it not on the scale of day to day happening,
It is ever young and eternal, it is ever-flowing.
Create your own world if you want to be counted amoung the living
The essence of past and present, life holds secret of human existence
Ask Farhad what life means
And you'll learn that it is a hard stone, an axe and a stream of milk, all at once
It submission, its shallow stream dries up
When free, life is a boundless sea
Although it is contained in a vessel of clay
It is characterized by dominance and sway
From the ocean, like a bubble, you have emerged
And in this world of deflation your mettle is tested
You are nothing more than a heap of clay when you are raw
When ripe, you are a sharp rapier,
He who wants to live and die for trugh
Must first acquire strength and power;

→

ख़ाम है जब तक कि है मिट्टी का इक अम्बार तू
पुख़्ता हो जाए तो है शमशेरे-बे ज़िनहार तू।

हो सदाक़त के लिए जिस दिल में मरने की तड़प
पहले अपने पैकरे-ख़ाकी में जां पैदा करे।
फूंक डाले यह ज़मीनो-आस्माने-मुस्तआर
और खाकिस्तर से आप अपना जहां पैदा करे।

ज़िंदगी की कुव्वते-पिनहां को कर दे आशकार
ता यह चिनगारी फ़रोगे-जावदां पैदा करे।
खाके मशरिक़ पर चमक जाए मिसाले-आफताब
ता बदख़्शां फिर वही लाले-गरां पैदा करे।

यह घड़ी महशर की है तू अरसा-ए-महशर में है
पेश कर गाफ़िल अमल कोई अगर दफ्तर में है।

Kham hai jab tak ki hai mitti ka ik ambar tu
Pukhta ho jaye to hai shamshere-be zinhar tu

Ho sadakat ke liye jis dil mein marne ki tarap
Pehle apne paikare-khaki mein jaan paida kare
Phoonk dale yeh zameeno asmane-mustair
Aur khakistar se aap apne jahan paida kare

Zindagee ki kuwate-pinha ko kar de aashkar
Ta yeh chingari pharoge-javadan paida kare
Khake-mashrik par chamak jaye misale-aaftab
Ta badakhshan phir vahi lale-garan paida kare

Yeh ghari mehshar ki hai tu arsa-e-mehshar mein hai
Pesh kar ghafil amal koi agar daftar mein hai

---

1. न मिटने वाले चमक, 2 अमूल्य मोती

Let him burn this borrowed earth, and sky
And out of the ashes, create his own world
The hidden strength of life must he find
And see the spark steady into eternal flame
Let him shine on the estern horizon like the sun
Until Badakhshan once again throws up the
priceless ruby
Towards heaven, his nocturnal lament let him send
And among the stars his confidants win
It's the day of judgmet, and you are in the midst
of it,
O careless one, show it now, if you have achieved
something sorthy and fit.

---

1. in Central Asia

हक़ीक़ते-हुस्न

ख़ुदा से हुस्न ने इक रोज़ यह सवाल किया
जहां में क्यों न मुझे तूने लाज़वाल[1] किया
मिला जवाब कि तस्वीरख़ाना है दुनिया
शबे-दराज़ अदम[2] का फ़साना है दुनिया
हुई है रंगे-तग़य्युर[3] से जब नमूद इसकी
वही हसीं है हक़ीक़त ज़वाल है जिसकी
कहीं क़रीब था, ये गुफ्तगू क़मर ने सुनी
फ़लक पे आम हुई, अख़्तरे-सहर[4] ने सुनी
सहर ने तारे से सुनकर सुनाई शबनम को
फ़लक की बात बता दी ज़मीं के महरम[5] को
फिर आए फूल के आंसू पयामे-शबनम से
कली का नन्हा-सा दिल ख़ून हो गया ग़म से॥
चमन से रोता हुआ मौसमे-बहार गया।
शबाब सैर को आया था, सोगवार[6] गया॥

Khuda se husn ne ik roz yeh sawal kiya
Jahan mein kyon na mujhe tune laazwaal kiya
Mila jawab ki tasveerkhana hai duniya
shabe-daraaz adam ka fasana hai duniya
Hui hai range-taghaiyur se jab namood iski
wahi haseen hai haqiqat zawaal hai jiski
Kahin Kareeb tha, ye guftgu qamar ne suni
Phalak pe aam hui, akhtare-sehar ne suni
Sehar ne taare se sunkar sunai shabnam ko
phalak ki baat bata di zameen ke mehram ko
Phir aaye phool ke aansu payame-shabnam se
kali ka nanha-sa dil khoon ho gaya gham se
Chaman se rota hua mausame-bahaar gaya
shabaab sair ko aaya tha, sogwar gaya

---

1. अमर 2. मृत्यु 3. परिवर्तनशीलता के रंग से 4. सुबह का तारा 5. भेदी 6. उदास

The Essence of Beauty

Beauty enquired of God one day
Why didn't you make me eternal?

God replied that this world is a picture gallery
It's a story of continuing mutability

Change is its essence
And only what decays, qualifies to be lovely.

Close by stood the moon, who heard this colloquy
Which soon spread to the entire sky and reached
the morning star

And the morning star, sharing it with the denizens
of the earth
Related it to the dew

The dew's report filled the flower's eyes with tears
And pierced with sorrow, the bud's delicate heart—

The springtime went from the garden weeping
And youth that came for a stroll, went into mourning.

गदाई

मैकदे में एक दिन एक रिंदे-ज़ीरक ने कहा
है हमारे शहर का वाली गदा-ए-बेहया[1]

ताज पहनाया है किसकी बेकुलाही ने उसे
किसकी उरियानी[2] ने बख़्शी है इसे ज़र्रीं क़बा

उसके आबे-लालगू की ख़ूने-दहकां[3] से कशीद
तेरे-मेरे खेत की मिट्टी है उसकी कीमिया

उसके नेमतख़ाने की हर चीज़ है मांगी हुई
देने वाला कौन है? मर्दे-ग़रीबो-बेनवा

मांगने वाला गदा है सदक़ा मांगे या ख़िराज
कोई माने या न माने मीर-ओ-सुलतां सब गदा

Maikade mein ek din rinde-zeerak ne kaha
hai humare shehar ka waali gada-e-behaya

Taaj pehnaya hai kiski bekulahi ne use
kiski uriyani ne bakhshi hai ise zarri qaba

Uske aabe-laalagun ki khoone-dehkaan se kasheed
tere-mere khet ki mitti hai uski kimiya

Uske ne'matkhane ki her cheez hai maangi hui
dene wala kaun hai ? marde-gharibo-benava

Maangne wala gada hai, sadqa mange ya khiraaj
koi maane ya na maane meer-o-sultaan sab gada

---

1. निर्लज्ज भिखारी 2. नग्नता 3. किसान का लहू

Beggary

A wise man one day said in the tavern
The ruler of our town is a shameless beggar

His crown only conceals his poverty
And his golden dress reveals only his nakedness

His red-coloured wine smacks of the peasants' blood
And his field are fertilized by your manure and mine

Every article in his luxury house, in fact, belongs
to us

who has given him all this?
Who, but the poor, voiceless men like you and me,

Anybody who takes from others, is a beggar
Whether he asks for alms or tribute

The kings and the nobles are beggars indeed
Even though they loot.

लबरेज़ है शराबे-हक़ीक़त से जामे हिंद
सब फ़लसफ़ी हैं ख़ित्ता-ए-मग़रिब के रामे हिंद

यह हिंदियों के फ़िक्रे-फ़लक-रस का है असर
रिफ़अत में आस्मां से भी ऊंचा है बामे-हिंद

इस देस में हुए हैं हज़ारों मलक सरिश्त[1]
मशहूर जिनके दम से है दुनिया में नामे-हिंद

है राम के वजूद पे हिंदोस्तां को नाज़
अहले-नज़र समझते हैं इसको इमामे-हिंद

एजाज़ इस चिराग़े-हिदायत का है यही
रोशनतर-अज़-सहर[2] है ज़माने में नामे-हिंद

तलवार का धनी था शुजाअत में फ़र्द था
पाकीज़गी में जोशे-मुहब्बत में फ़र्द[3] था

Labrez hai sharabe-haqiqat se jaame hind
sab phalsafin hain khitta-e-maghrib ke rame hind

Yeh hindiyon ke phikre-phalak ras ka hai asar
rifát mein aasmaan se bhi ooncha hai baame-hind

Is des mein hue hain hazaron malak-sarisht
mashhoor jinke dam se hai duniya mein naame-hind

Hai Ram ke wajood pe hindostan ko naaz
ahle-nazar samajhte hain isko imaame hind

Aijaz is chirage-hidayat ka hai yahi
roshantar-az-sehar hai zamane mein naame-hind

Talwar ka dhani tha shujáet mein phard tha
pakizagi mein joshe-muhabbat mein phard tha

---

1. देवता के स्वभाव वाले 2. सुबह से अधिक रोशन 3. बेजोड़

Rama

India's cup is overflowing with the wine of wisdom.
The philosophers of the West all acknowledge
its might.

The loftiness of our thought, it is
That lifts us high above the sky.

Hundred of angelic spirits we have produced
Who, to this earth have lustre lent.

And it is to our credit that Ram was born here,
For the knowledgeable know that he is a
leader great.

It is because of the light of wisdom that our evening
are brighter than the morning elsewhere.

In valour outstanding, in swordsmanship grand.
In love and piety unique would our Ram stand.

दुआ

या रब दिले-मुस्लिम को वह ज़िंदा तमन्ना दे
जो क़ल्ब को गर्मा दे, जो रूह को तड़पा दे

फिर वादी-ए-फ़ारां के हर ज़र्रे को चमका दे
फिर शौक़े तमाशा दे, फिर ज़ौक़े तक़ाज़ा दे

महरूमे-तमाशा को फिर दीदा-ए-बीना दे
देखा है जो कुछ मैंने औरों को भी दिखला दे

भटके हुए आहू को फिर सुए-हरम ले चल
इस शहर के ख़ूगर को फिर वुसअते-सहरा दे

पैदा दिले-वीरां में फ़िर शोरिशे-महशर कर
इस महमिले-ख़ाली को फिर शाहिदे-लैला दे

इस दौर की ज़ुलमत में हर क़ल्बे-परेशां को

→

Yaa Rub diley muslim ko woh zinda tamanna de
jo qalb ko garma de, jo rooh ko tarpa de

Phir wadi-e-pharaan ke her zarrey ko chamkade
phir shoqe-tamasha de, phir zauqe-taqaza de

Mehroome tamasha ko phir deeda-e-beena de
dekha hai jo kuchh maine auron ko bhi dikhla de

Bhatke hue aahu ko phri sue-harum le chal
is shehar ke khugar ko phir vusáte-sehra de

Paida diley-viraan mein phir shorishe-mehshar kar
is mehmele-khali ko phir shahide-laila de

Is daur ku zulmat mein her qalbe-pareshan ko

A Prayer

Fill the Muslims, O Lord, with a desire so fervent
That warms up the heart, stirs their soul

And brightens up every speck of dust in the
Faoan valley;
Give them once again the restless eye that longs
for more;

To those deprived of sight, grant a piercing eye
And let them see what I have seen;

Lead the wandering bird to the sanctuary again
And let the townsmen the vastness of the
desert see;

And create in the desolate heart the stir of the
judgment day
And let Laila be seated on the letter again

→

वह दाग़े-मुहब्बत दे जो चांद को शर्मा दे
रिफ़अत में मक़ासिद को हमगोशे-सुरैया कर

खुद्दारी-ए-साहिल दे आज़ादी-ए-दरिया दे
बेलौस मुहब्बत हो, बेबाक सदाक़त हो

सीनों में उजाला कर दिल सूरते मीना दे
एहसास इनायत कर आसारे-मुसीबत का
इमरोज़ की शोरिश में अंदेशा-ए-फ़र्दा दे

मैं बुलबुले-नाला हूँ इक उजड़े गुलिस्तां का
तासीर का सायल हूँ, मोहताज को दाता दे

woh Daaghe-muhabbat de jo chand ko sharma de
Rifát mein maqasid ko humgoshe-suraiyha kar

khuddari-e-sahil de azadi-e-dariya de
Belos muhabbat ho, bebaak sadaqat ho

seenon mein ujala kar dil surate meena de
Ahsaas inayat kar aasaare musibat ka
imroz ki shorish mein andesha-e-pharda de

Main bulbule-naalaan hun ik ujare gulistaan ka
taseer ka saayal hun, mohtaaj ko daata de

In the darkness of this age, grant every heart
the glow of love
That outshines the moon above

In loftiness, let their aim be as high as Pleidas
And to the beauty of the shore, the vastness of the
ocean grant

Let their love be selfless, unbounded the truth,
Light up their hearts and grant them foresight
Of the calamity that may befall tomorrow.

I am the lament of the nightingale in the garden
ruined, O God
Grant the prayer of a poor beggar, my Lord.

फूल

तुझे क्यों फ़िक्र है ऐ गुल! दिले-सद चाक बुलबुल की
तू अपने पैरहन के चाक तो पहले रफ़ू कर ले

तमन्ना आबरू की हो अगर गुलज़ारे-हस्ती[1] में
तो कांटों में उलझकर ज़िंदगी करने की ख़ू[2] कर ले

नहीं ये शाने-खुद्दारी, चमन से तोड़कर तुझको,
कोई दस्तार[3] में रख ले, कोई ज़ेबे-गुलू[4] कर ले

Tujhe kyon phikr hai ae gul ! diley sad chaak bulbul ki
tu apne pairhan ke chaak to pehle rafu kar le

Tamanna aabru ki ho agar gulzare-hasti mein
to kanton mein ulajhkar zindgi karne ki khu kar le

Nahin ye shaane-khuddari, chaman se torkar tujhko
koi dastaar mein rakh le, koi zebey-gulu kar le

---

1. संसार 2. स्वभाव 3. पगड़ी 4. गले की शोभा

The Flower

Why are you so bothered, O flower, about the barbed
heart of the nightingale
You had better stitch up the holes in your own
apparel first,

If you indeed wish to live with honour in the garden
of life
Side by side with the thorns let you learn to live,

It is not proper that somebody should pluck you
from the garden
And garland himself or tuck you in his turban.

फ़लसफ़ा और मज़हब

यह आफ़ताब क्या यह सिपहरे-बरीं[1] है क्या
समझा नहीं तसलसुले-शामो-सहर[2] को मैं

अपने वतन में हूं कि ग़रीब-उल-दियार[3] हूं?
डरता हूं देख-देखके इस दश्तो-दर को मैं

खुलता नहीं मेरे सफ़रे ज़िंदगी का राज़
लाऊं कहां से बंदा-ए-साहिब-नज़र को मैं?

हैरां है 'बूअली' कि मैं आया कहां से हूं?
'रूमी' यह सोचता है कि जाऊं किधर को मैं?

"जाता हूं थोड़ी दूर हर इक तेज़ रौ के साथ
पहचानता नहीं हूं अभी राहबर को मैं"

Yeh aaftaab kya yeh siphare-barin hai kya
samjha nahin tasalsule-shaamo-sehar ko main

Apne vatan mein hoon ki gharib-ul-diyaar hoon
darta hun dekh-dekhke is dashto-dar ko main

Khulta nahin mere safar-e-zindgi ka raaz
laaun kahan se banda-e-sahib-nazar ko main

Hairan hai 'buáli' ki main aaya kahan se hoon
'Rumi' yeh sochta hai ki jaaun kidhar ko main

'Jata hoon thori door her ik rehro ke saath
pehchanta nahin hoon abhi raahber ko main

---

1. ऊंचा आकाश 2. सुबह-शाम का अनुक्रम 3. परदेसी

Philosophy and Religion

What is the sun, what is this sky so high?
I have not been able to comprehend the sequence
of day and night

Am I home or in an alien land?
I'm scared at the sight of this vast expanse;

I cannot solve the puzzle of my life
I possess not the insight for that;

Boo Ali knows not from where he came
Rumi does not know his destination;

With every traveller, a few steps I go
My guide as yet I do not know.

चांद

मेरे वीराने से कोसों दूर है तेरा वतन
है मगर दरिया-ए-दिल तेरी कशिश से मौजज़न[1]

क़स्द[2] *किस महफ़िल का है? आता है किस महफ़िल से तू?*
ज़र्द-रू शायद हुआ रंजे-रहे-मंज़िल से तू

आफ़रीनिश[3] *से सरापा नूर तू, ज़ुल्मत*[4] *हूं मैं*
इस सियाह-रोज़ी पे लेकिन तेरा हम-क़िस्मत हूं मैं
आह! मैं जलता हूँ सोज़े इश्तयाक़े दीद से
तू सरापा सोज़ दाग़े मंन्नते ख़ुरशीद से

एक हल्क़े पर अगर कायम तेरी रफ़्तार है
मेरी गर्दिश भी मिसाले-गर्दिशे-परकार है

ज़िंदगी की रह में सरगरदां[5] *है तू हैरां हूं मैं*
तू फ़रोज़ा महफ़िले-हस्ती में है, सोज़ां हूं मैं

मैं रहे-मंज़िल में हूं, तू भी रहे-मंज़िल में है
तेरी महफ़िल में जो ख़ामोशी है मेरे दिल में है

→

Mere veerane se koson door hai tera vatan
hai magar dariya-e-dil teri kashish se maujzan

Qarad kis mehfil ka hai ? aata hai kis mehfil se tu
zard-ru shayad hua ranje-rahe-manzil se tu

Aafarinish se sarapa noor tu, zulmat hoon main
is siyaah-rozi pe lekin tera hum-qismat hoon main

Ah! main jalta hun soze-ishtyaaqe deed se
Tu saraapa soz daghi mannate khursheed se

Ek halqe per agar qayam teri raftaar hai
meri gardish bhi misale-gardishe-parkaar hai

Zindgi ki rah mein sargardan hai tu hairan hoon main
tu faroza mehfile-hasti mein hai, sozan hoon main

Main rahe manzil mein hun, tu bhi rahe-manzil mein hai
teri mehfil mein jo khamoshi hai mere dil mein hai

---

1. तरंगित 2. संकल्प 3. सृष्टिकाल 4. अंधकार 5. घूम रहा है

The Moon

Your home is leagues away from where I live
Yet my heart leaps up as I see your loveliness like
the ocean does

What is your destination, where did you set out from
Perhaps the weariness of the journey has turned
you pale;

From the day of creation, you are light incarnate
though and darkness I,
I burn with a passion, for my beloved sight, I pine
As you are burning with desire and beg the sun
for light,

If you are bound to go round and round in a circle
My life too is moving like the hand of a compass

To such a course I am condemned much like you
You are shining though in your bright company,
I am burning,

I too have a long way to go before I reach my goal
like you
My heart too in miniature mirrors the silence
surrounding you,

→

तू तलब-ख़ू[1] है तो मेरा भी यही दस्तूर है
चांदनी है नूर तेरा, इश्क़ मेरा नूर है

अंजुमन है एक मेरी भी जहां रहता हूं मैं
बज़्म में अपनी अगर यकता है तू, तनहा हूं मैं

मेह्र का परतौ तेरे हक़ में है पैग़ामे-अजल
मह्व कर देता है मुझको जल्वा-ए-हुस्ने अज़ल

फिर भी ऐ माहे-मुबीं! मैं और हूं तू और है
दर्द जिस पहलू में उठता हो वो पहलू और है

गर्चे मैं ज़ुल्मत-सरापा हूं, सरापा नूर तू
सैकड़ों मंज़िल है ज़ौके-आगही[2] से दूर तू

जो मेरी हस्ती का मक़सद है तुझे मालूम है
ये चमक वो है, जबीं जिससे तेरी महरूम है

Tu talab-khu hai to mera bhi yahi dastoor hai
chandni hai noor tera, ishq mera noor hai

Anjuman hai ek meri bhi jahan rehta hoon main
bazm mein apni agar yakta hai tu, tanha hoon main

Mehai ka partoo tere huq mein hai paighame-ajal
mahi kar deta hai mujhko jalwa-e-husne azal

Phir bhi ae maahe-mubin ! main aur hoon tu aur hai
dard jis pehlu mein uthta ho woh pehlu aur hai

Garche mein zulmat-sarapa hun, sarapa noor tu
sainkaron manzil hai zauqe-aagahi se door tu

Jo meri hasti ka maqsad hai tujhe maloom hai
ye chamak woh hai, jabeen jisse teri mehroom hai

You are a seeker, so am I
Love is my light, as silvery glow is yours

I am lonely even in company much like your
loneliness in the sky

Like the light of the sun that heralds your death
The glow of eternity, me in amazement drowns—

And yet O shining moon, you are not me and I am
not you
For, you possess not the heart that aches

Even though you are an embodiment of light and
I am darkness incarnate,
You experience not the passion for knowledge

The purpose of my life you surely know
But that which I experience, you lack that glow

परिंदे की फ़रियाद

आता है याद मुझको गुज़रा हुआ ज़माना
वो बाग़ की बहारें वो सबका चहचहाना

आज़ादियां कहां वो अब अपने घोंसले की
अपनी ख़ुशी से आना अपनी ख़ुशी से जाना

लगती है चोट दिल पर, आता है याद जिस दम
शबनम के आंसुओं पर कलियों का मुस्कराना

वो प्यारी-प्यारी सूरत वो कामनी-सी मूरत
आबाद जिसके दम से था मेरा आशियाना

आती नहीं सदाएं उसकी मेरे क़फ़स में
होती मेरी रिहाई ऐ काश मेरे बस में

Aata hai yaad mujhko guzra hua zamana
woh baagh ki baharein woh sabka chehchahana

Azadiyan kahan woh ab apne ghonsale ki
apni khushi se aana apni khushi se jaana

Lagti hai chot dil per, aata hai yaad jis dam
shabnam ke aansuon per kaliyon ka muskurana

Woh pyari-pyari surat woh kaamni-si murat
aabaad jiske dam se tha mera aashiyana

Aati nahin sadaen uski mere qafas mein
hoti meri rihaai ae kaash mere bas mein!

The Cry of the Bird

How I miss the times past
Miss the garden in spring, miss that chirping around
I miss very much the freedom of my nest
Which I could leave and return to at will
The smiling buds, the weeping dew—
Wherever I remember the lovely sight
That sustained my life
A knife, I feel, passing through my heart.

In vain do I long for those sights and sounds, in the cage here
How I wish I could be free again!

→

क्या बदनसीब हूं मैं घर को तरस रहा हूं
साथी तो हैं वतन में, मैं क़ैद में पड़ा हूं

आई बहार, कलियां फूलों की हंस रही हैं
मैं इस अंधेरे घर में क़िस्मत को रो रहा हूं

इस क़ैद का इलाही! दुखड़ा किसे सुनाऊं
डर है यहीं क़फ़स में मैं ग़म से मर न जाऊं

जब से चमन छुटा है यह हाल हो गया है
दिल ग़म को खा रहा है, ग़म दिल को खा रहा है

गाना इसे समझकर खुश हों न सुनने वाले
दुखते हुए दिलों की फ़र्याद यह सदा है

आज़ाद मुझको कर दे ओ क़ैद करने वाले
मैं बेज़बान हूँ क़ैदी, तू छोड़कर दुआ ले

Kya badnaseeb hun main ghar ko taras raha hun
sathi to hain vatan mein, main qaid mein parahun

Aai bahaar kaliyan phoolon ki hans rahi hain
main is andhere ghar mein qismat ko ro raha hun

Is qaid ka ilaahi dukhra kise sunaun
dar hai yahin qafas mein main gham se mar ne jaaun

Jab se chaman chhuta hai yeh haal ho gaya hai
dil gham ko kha raha hai, gham dil ko kha raha hai

Gana ise samajhkar khush ho na sunne wale
dukhte hue dilon ki faryad yeh sada hai

Azad mujhko kar de O qaid karne wale
main bezaban hun qaidi, tu chhorkar dua le

How wretched I am that I cannot go home
While my companions are free and here I am in
the prison,
There is spring around and flowers bloom everywhere
While I curse my lot in this house of darkness here,

I am afraid I shall die of sorrow in this prison.
O God, with whom shall I share the sorrow
of incarceration!

Since the day I have been exiled from the garden
My heart is a hostage to sorrow, my grief is
tearing it apart!

This is a cry from a stricken heart,
Be not happy, O listener, take it not for a song

A tongue-tied prisoner I am
Free me, O my captor
And I shall bless you forever.

चांद और सितारे

डरते-डरते दमे-सहर से
तारे कहने लगे क़मर[1] से

नज़ारे रहे वही फ़लक पर
हम थक भी गये चमक-चमक कर

काम अपना है सुबह-ओ-शाम चलना
चलना, चलना, मुदाम[2] चलना

बेताब है इस जहां की हर शै
कहते हैं जिसे सकूं, नहीं है

होगा कभी ख़त्म यह सफ़र क्या

→

Darte-darte dame-sehar se
taare kehne lage qamar se

Nazare rahe wahin falak per
hum thak bhi gaye chamak-chamak kar

Kaam apna hai subah-o-sham chalna
chalna, chalna, mudaam chalna

Betaab hai is jahan ki her shey
kehte hain jise sakun nahin hai

Hoga kabhi khatm yeh safar kya

---

1. चांद 2. निरंतर

The Moon and the Stars

Trembling at the approach of dawn
The stars to the moon said:

Morning and evening we are moving through the sky
Eternal wandering is our lot

While the sky beside us changeless lies;
Shining on it, we are tired indeed;

Why does the world know, no peace,
Why is everything restless here?

Will this journey ever end?

→

मंज़िल कभी आयेगी नज़र क्या?
कहने लगा चांद, हमनशीनो!

ऐ गज़रअ-ए-शब[1] के ख़ोशाचीनो[2]!
जुंबिश से है ज़िन्दगी जहां की

यह रस्म क़दीम[3] है यहां की
इस रह में मुक़ाम बेमहल है

पोशीदा क़रार में अज़ल है
चलने वाले निकल गए हैं

जो ठहरे ज़रा, कुचल गए हैं

manzil kabhi aayegi nazar kya
Kehne laga chand, humnashino

ae gazar-e-shab ke khoshachino
Zumbish se hai zindagi jahan ki

yeh rasm qadeem hai yahan ki
Is rah mein muqaam bemehal hai

poshida qarar mein azal hai
Chalne wale nikal gaye hain

jo thehare zara, kuchal gaye hain

---

1. रात की खेती 2. बालियां चुनने वालों 3. प्राचीन

Shall we ever our destination reach?
"You, who glean the field of night, my comrades dear"
Replied the moon
"Only in change, the beauty of life lies"
Rest is its anti-thesis

Only those who move, their goal attain

And the ones who stop, live and die in vain.

❑❑❑